THE LEAN EXPERT

Educating and Elevating Lean Practitioners Throughout Your Organization

Joseph Niederstadt

THE LEAN EXPERT

Educating and Elevating Lean Practitioners Throughout Your Organization

CRC Press
Taylor & Francis Group
Boca Raton   London   New York

CRC Press is an imprint of the
Taylor & Francis Group, an **informa** business

A PRODUCTIVITY PRESS BOOK

CRC Press
Taylor & Francis Group
6000 Broken Sound Parkway NW, Suite 300
Boca Raton, FL 33487-2742

Printed on acid-free paper
Version Date: 20141009

International Standard Book Number-13: 978-1-4822-5365-8 (Paperback)

Visit the Taylor & Francis Web site at
http://www.taylorandfrancis.com

and the CRC Press Web site at
http://www.crcpress.com

I would like to dedicate this work to the hundreds and hundreds of people who chose to make the commitment and persevered to "graduate" to a Lean Discipline Expert! They have been from all different levels in many organizations. I have watched these people apply their training and skill sets of their particular Lean Discipline to coach and lead others to implement and sustain what they teach. I always find it amazing to watch the Lean Discipline Experts grow stronger in technique and confidence with each application. They have helped their companies in Safety, Quality, Cost, Productivity, and Cash Flow to become competitors in a global marketplace, and that is no easy task. But it wasn't an easy task to become a Lean Discipline Expert either. They are huge assets not only to their companies, but to themselves; they can take this education and apply it anywhere their paths take them. They all have truly garnered my utmost respect and admiration for their achievement of becoming a Lean Discipline Expert, as well as for their accomplishments in applying their particular disciplines in the workplace!

Contents

Preface

I believe that it is well understood that companies on a Lean journey have, as part of their Lean system, a House of Lean that shows the foundations for their Lean system as well as some basic core principles. I have also seen some that use Lean Pyramids that accomplish the same thing, but for the most part, the House of Lean graphic is most commonly utilized. The Lean House lays out the systematic approach a company will use in the Lean journey it has embarked upon. It is also a great visual control that provides an understanding of the Lean path to anyone whenever and wherever it is shown.

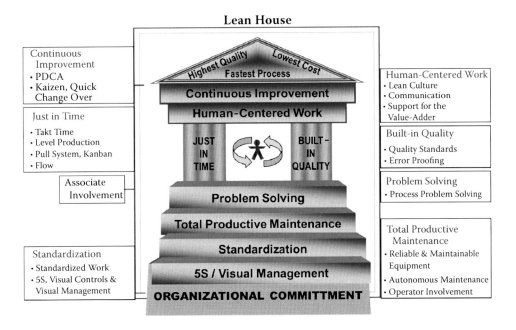

In the material that follows, I will refer to nine of the core principles as they relate to the process of creating Lean Discipline Experts for your business. These core principles are

5S–Visual Management
Value Stream Mapping
Standard Work (Cyclical and Noncyclical)
Total Productive Maintenance
Quick Changeover
Error Proofing
Process Problem Solving
Material Management
Continuous Improvement

Two additional portions of the House of Lean example above that I would like to bring to your attention are Human-Centered Work and Associate Involvement. These are all about the people without whom you cannot provide a quality product for your customers. While I was mentored by several Toyota Senseis, it was hammered into my brain that these attributes of a Lean journey are critical for success. Toyota expects all their people to be Lean change agents on a daily basis. If the entire workforce is not clearly empowered and engaged, how is that supposed to happen?

I have seen several plants where the management team was well schooled in Lean tools and implemented them very effectively. But when members of that Management Team began to leave, through promotion or some other reason, what *they* had implemented fell apart in a short period of time because they had not engaged or empowered their workforce in the implementation process! Since the workforce had no ownership in any of the processes, they really had no reason to challenge why the business was no longer following a procedure.

There is another danger I have witnessed many times at businesses that claim they are implementing Lean. You may have heard of this before; it is called *cherry-picking*. That is when the management team or a member of management decides to implement only certain aspects of the Lean House. This generally is a basic lack of understanding that the Lean disciplines overlap and interact with each other. They are not stand-alone tools!

As a young supervisor in the automotive manufacturing business, I very quickly learned from my peers that knowledge is power, and as long as you did not share your knowledge with others, you were valuable to the company. Unfortunately, it was the normal and accepted business practice at the facility where I was working, and that mentality permeated all through the organization, including the senior leadership. In fact, that same thinking was used in the decision-making process for people advancement! Do you remember your training on the different forms of waste? Consider the eighth waste—untouched human potential, the associates!

Thank goodness we have come a long way with our understanding on how business needs have changed. We now have to compete globally, even with mom-and-pop shops located across the globe. Thank goodness we now have Lean leaders and Lean thinkers who understand that knowledge is not power unless it is shared throughout the organization. This knowledge sharing gives a business a competitive advantage in a global market simply by having our associates understand what our customer wants, how we can provide the customer with a quality product, and how we can be cost competitive. Imagine having an army of Lean change agents! Well, that is exactly why Toyota and some other businesses that have implemented a true Lean business system are very successful in competing in global markets today.

The Lean Discipline Expert process beautifully supports and requires associate involvement at all levels. You will see where and how the nine principles overlap and interact. By engaging and empowering various levels of associates throughout your organization, you will provide strength and ownership for your business and, most importantly, your associates! My experience in using this process in multiple businesses is that the people welcome it and embrace it. They are eager to be involved in the success of their employer, and they also realize that it helps secure their jobs against competitors.

Chapter 1

Introduction to the Lean Discipline Expert Process

The main purpose of the Lean Discipline Expert process is to provide a method with defined steps for the development of Lean Discipline Resource People, leading to achievement of "expert status" in their specific Lean discipline. This may sound simple, but I assure you that it is a tough but rewarding process to go through and complete.

I know there may be some Lean purists out there who may have some angst when I use the term *expert*. So let's see how Webster's Dictionary* defines the term. The Webster's Dictionary definitions are as follows: "having, involving, or displaying special skill or knowledge derived from training or experience." This is exactly what this process is all about: training and experience to develop special skill sets!

You should also take comfort in the fact that I understand education and know that learning is an ongoing process, whether you are considered a Lean expert or a Lean practitioner. That it is how it should be: Our minds should always be open to new concepts, tools, or methodologies. But I guarantee that if you trust in and follow the Lean Discipline Expert process correctly, your candidates will have a level of expertise in their particular subject matter equal to most of the Lean Practitioners in the business world today. They will not only have a great deal of confidence in their knowledge, but will be your company's go-to person related to that particular principle for guidance, workshops, and general questions on implementation. They will bring strength to your Lean journey and your organization.

---

* www.webstersonline.com

Now let's proceed to the introduction on how this process works. In the Preface to this book, I mentioned nine specific Lean disciplines for this process. Each Lean discipline will need a Champion to act as a mentor for the various candidates. Normally, this is a staff or department head, and sometimes the Champion may have more than one Lean discipline.

Next, there needs to be a pool developed that consists of both *salaried* and *hourly* probable candidates. The best way to sustain the Lean Discipline Expert process is to have one salaried and one hourly candidate as Lean Discipline Experts per discipline. This approach clearly demonstrates that everyone supports the Lean Discipline Expert process and that all are working toward the same goals. In Chapter 2, I will further explain the best method I know to go about creating the pool of potential candidates for becoming a Lean Discipline Expert.

The process is based on checklists and feedback that includes (but is not limited to) utilizing mandatory reading materials from your Lean Library (see Chapter 13), participating in teams to identify and implement best practices, actively participating in workshops both on and off site, and eventually facilitating workshops. Now that may sound simple, but I can assure you that this process is not only an investment in your people, but also your company and the future of both. It requires a commitment of time and some financial resources to achieve becoming a Lean Discipline Expert. From my experience in utilizing this process, it takes about two years for a candidate to complete the entire process to become a Lean Discipline Expert of one Lean discipline! So you should be able to surmise that this is no simple process of merely checking a box and then moving on.

Similar to a formal education system, the Lean Discipline Expert process is divided into four distinct achievement points:

- Lean Discipline Apprentice
- Lean Discipline Generalist
- Lean Discipline Specialist
- Lean Discipline Expert

For the *Lean Discipline Apprentice* section, candidates will complete training in Lean overview as well as specific subject matter overview, and this will require an 80% to 90% level of support and mentoring. Upon completion of the Lean Discipline Apprentice process, candidates will have achieved a basic understanding of their Lean discipline.

For the *Lean Discipline Generalist* section, candidates will learn about the bigger picture of Lean. They will understand and apply Lean vision and mission strategies, complete comprehensive training related to their Lean disciplines (and other Lean disciplines that overlap their subject), and learn to support implementation with mentoring assistance to guarantee proper implementation (requiring 40% to 80% level of support and mentoring). Upon completion of the Lean Discipline Generalist process, the candidates will be able to implement their Lean discipline with assistance.

For the *Lean Discipline Specialist* section, the candidates have already achieved the title of Lean Discipline Generalist for their particular Lean discipline, and completed repeated applications of their subject matter to enhance their personal knowledge and expertise. In this section they will achieve the skill sets to facilitate others in the application of their particular Lean discipline (requiring 0% to 40% level of support and mentoring). Upon completion of the Lean Discipline Specialist process, candidates will be able to implement and sustain their particular Lean discipline.

For the *Lean Discipline Expert* section, the candidates will develop Lean strategies, create a Master Schedule and initiate activities for supporting goals and objectives, and complete a Train-the-Trainer class. Additionally, the candidate will achieve facilitation skills to teach, communicate, guide, and lead Lean discipline overview training as well as comprehensive subject-matter training. They will initiate and lead subject-matter activity at an existing site or organization and have the ability to apply their Lean discipline expertise to the development of new processes, new products, or even new facilities. Upon completion of the Lean Discipline Expert process, the candidates will be able to lead, identify, teach, implement, and sustain their Lean discipline with minimal support or even without assistance.

The outcome of becoming a Lean Discipline Expert is a big accomplishment and should be treated as such. People who achieve this status should be recognized at the highest level and be given a certificate of accomplishment (example provided on the CRC Press website http://www.crcpress. com/product/isbn/9781482253658 under the downloads tab). Their personnel file should also reflect that they have become a Lean Discipline Expert in their particular Lean discipline, and some form of trophy or plaque should be presented along with a one-time monetary reward (determined at either the corporate or plant level).

As we are talking about nine different Lean disciplines with two candidates each, a tracking mechanism is needed to monitor candidate progress. I have included, under the downloads tab of the book's website (http://www.crcpress.com/product/isbn/9781482253658), an example of a method for doing just that, but if you prefer to make your own, feel free to do so.

Chapter 2

Selecting Lean Discipline Expert Candidates

Based upon my experience, the best way to begin creating your pool of probable candidates is a meeting facilitated by the Human Resource department with representatives from all the various departments such as Manufacturing, Engineering (Mechanical, Industrial, etc.), Quality, Production Control and Logistics, Purchasing, Maintenance, etc. The purpose of this meeting is for the various representatives to nominate employees, both salaried and hourly, for the Lean Discipline Expert process. Let's discuss some advice for selecting Lean Discipline Expert candidates and some tips on what attributes to look for as well as some tips on what to watch out for.

Your Lean system provides the power that should be driving the process of performance improvements in your workplace that differentiate your organization from your competitors'. For example, the focus is normally on Safety, Quality, Cost, Delivery, Environment, and Employee Involvement.

Lean Discipline Experts (LDEs) provide the inertia for your Lean system. Knowledge is power, and your Lean system really has the opportunity to move forward when all of your associates are knowledgeable and fully engaged in Lean. Thus the selection of LDEs is paramount to the success of your Lean journey.

I use the word *probable* in association with candidates because they will need to be volunteers to become Lean Discipline Experts (LDEs). The process is not designed for candidates to receive financial compensation for acting as a Lean Discipline Expert, nor is becoming a Lean Discipline Expert a full-time job. The candidates need to be willing to go through the Lean

Discipline Expert process and function as the go-to person for that particular Lean discipline in addition to their normal duties. This may include answering general questions for staff members and hourly associates alike, facilitating workshops, reporting results to staff at every level, and in larger organizations, formal reporting to corporate representatives.

What I have learned is that it takes more than just enthusiasm to make a good Lean Discipline Expert. Many people can become a master in one or more Lean disciplines, but they can't clearly convey that knowledge to others. LDEs must be able to teach and coach. This teaching is to be done in a group setting. These experts must be able to effectively handle group dynamics, organize thoughts and ideas, keep the learning process moving forward, adjust their pace as needed, answer difficult questions, and condense complex concepts into simple, standardized components. They also must have the ability to do this in a manufacturing or business process setting.

I would like to share with you, based upon my experience, some of the characteristics of a strong Lean Discipline Expert (LDE) candidate. I think it is very import that you should understand that most of the best LDE candidates will come directly from Gemba, the place where the work is done, because there they have hands-on experience. Keep an open mind that this could be either a manufacturing or business process environment. Although eagerness and passion for the Lean discipline expertise is important, some other factors are essential to be successful in this role.

First and foremost is the ability to *clearly* communicate. Communicating, teaching, and coaching topics like Value Stream Mapping, Standard Work (Cyclical and Noncyclical), and Total Productive Maintenance is a difficult job. This is especially true when there is resistance to change in the workplace environment. All cultural change initiatives are challenging, but my experience has been that most companies have many associates who have given their very best over the years.

Generally speaking, hopefully these people have watched the company grow and become immensely successful. There may be instances where they have also lived through some changes in company direction that were not as successful or changes that were implemented but not sustained. The latter is very frustrating for the workforce and usually creates a situation where the need for change is understood. In some cases, working for a company has become a family-oriented value involving multiple generations. Sometimes people will not understand why we need to change our work habits and patterns. If we have been successful in the past, what's broken? Why change? These types of thoughts can be the cornerstone of resistance. The LDE, along with other organizational leaders, must be able to communicate why change is the only constant in our global competitive environment and make skeptics understand the upsides of change. Additionally the LDEs must be able to convey and include a "what's in it for me" (commonly referred to as WIIFM) response.

The LDEs must believe in themselves, their potential, and their abilities. This self-confidence is essential when it comes to delivering messages. It reflects in voice tone and quality, enthusiasm for the subject matter, and activities that encourage the complete interaction of the participants. This self-confidence must be contagious enough to motivate others to modify their behaviors and implement Lean processes in their work areas. It isn't easy standing in front of others and putting your reputation on the line; it takes courage to take that risk. Even after all the years of leadership training delivered in high schools and colleges, churches, social groups, and even in courses like Dale Carnegie, public speaking remains the number one fear for many (a fear greater than death itself for some!). When selecting an LDE, please keep in mind that there is a difference between being a self-confident individual and being an egomaniac. Arrogance and displays of knowledge power or positional power have no place in a teaching setting.

The ability to deal with uncertainty is another crucial trait. No one has all the answers. From my personal experience, I have learned that participants will ask questions that I hadn't anticipated, and I may not have the answer at hand. Knowing how to deal with these situations and knowing how to use the knowledge in the classroom is a necessary response tool.

Lean Discipline Experts must be skilled at more than just presenting. The role of the LDE is to teach, and teaching requires working with the group and with individuals within the group to ensure that knowledge has been conveyed. Workplace teaching is not like a university lecture. Adults in the workplace must understand why they are at the learning session, what is expected of them after the session, and why this learning is essential to their jobs. In the workplace, the full absorption of the teaching must occur through practice, activities, and exercises. Less than 10% of all participants learn best through listening to a presentation or lecture, so the LDE must have the skill to utilize techniques such as flipcharts, whiteboards, PowerPoint, hands-on events, and more that engage the participants and make the lesson impactful.

Just as people and personalities are different, not just stamped cutouts, there isn't just one template for selecting an LDE. It comes down to a combination of personal traits, drives, and abilities. The following bullet lists should act as a guide to provide some further assistance on what to look for during your selection process. Interviewing the candidates, clarifying the LDE role and responsibilities, and determining the candidate's motivation to become an LDE allow you to establish a firm groundwork for selection.

Bear in mind that not everyone can be a Lean Discipline Expert. There are roles that will be needed at the Lean Discipline Apprentice (LDA), Lean Discipline Generalist (LDG), and Lean Discipline Specialist (LDS) levels. Gratitude and recognition of the contributions at each level must be communicated. Careful preparation and selection will produce LDEs who will not only learn the content and be able to pass the regimen of facilitation skills the first time around, but most importantly they will pass those skills on to others.

Demonstrated traits:
- Strong and vibrant communicator
- Ability to solve problems and seek out answers both during and after the program
- Adaptable, with the ability to think on one's feet
- Fair, with a demonstrated ability to shelve personal biases
- Organized, commonsense thinker
- Enjoys people, but not a social butterfly
- Poised and willing to present materials to others in a stand-up setting
- A learner, someone who has shown that, although the individual is the teacher, the group and the teacher can learn from one another
- Calm demeanor, not easily rattled, but someone who brings energy to the subject
- Exhibits maturity and impartiality
- Alert to observe the group process, checking on the transfer of learning while working to deliver the subject matter content
- Ability and willingness to travel to other locations and teach unfamiliar people

LDE selection cautions:
- Grandstanders, those who truly believe they know it all or want attention from many people
- Those who want the position for the rewards or the power of the position

- People for whom stand-up speaking provokes fear, embarrassment, or aversion
- Communicators who don't speak clearly or can't explain an issue or circumstances using several examples
- Disjointed individuals who have not demonstrated the ability to plan ahead and then work the plan
- Slide readers—those who can read a set of slides but don't have the skills to handle a group of people or who are not versatile enough to work without the slides (These people typically show no joy in teaching and lack energy when delivering content.)
- Eager beginners—those who want to teach but have not had enough seasoning (experience, displayed maturity, etc.)

Chapter 3

LDE Checklist, Status Look-Across Chart, Facilitation Feedback Form, and Recognition

As you review each Lean Discipline Checklist, you will notice that there is extensive classroom and hands-on training for the candidate on their particular Lean discipline. You will also notice additional training in Lean disciplines that cross over into their particular subject. The presumption I have made is that if you truly have a Lean system in place, it will contain training modules for all of these basic Lean disciplines. If for some reason you find yourself short of a training package or two, you will want to contact your local or state colleges to see what they have to offer to make up for anything lacking. Many colleges today offer a variety of courses geared toward Lean in a work environment.

During your initial discussion on implementing the Lean Discipline Expert process into your company, it is very important to review each of the Lean Discipline Expert checklists (see Table 3.1) and agree, right up front, with the designation of those who are authorized to sign off on the various sections of each checklist.

The checklist forms that I have supplied under the downloads tab of the CRC Press website for the book (http://www.crcpress.com/product/isbn/9781482253658) engages the trainee, the Lean Manager/Coordinator (this can be corporate, divisional, or plant levels), and the Plant Manager.

Table 3.1   LDE Checklist Document

Your Company Logo Here	Your Lean System Initials Here	Title: Training Overview Checklist for CI LDEs	Date: August 14, 2014	Rev: 1.0	Page: Page 2 of 10	Document No.: XXX-CI-7202 Approved by: HR Manager

Starting Date: ____/____/____   Trainee's Name:_____

(Please Print Legibly)

Training Overview Checklist for CI LDEs

This training checklist is to be utilized in training Continuous Improvement LDEs. Each item needs to be covered by the support personnel listed. As the trainee completes an item, the trainee (T) initials and dates the item. The Lean Manager/Coordinator (LMC) and Plant Manager (PM) initial to indicate that the training is completed.

When a section is completed, the trainee, the Lean Manager/Coordinator, and the Plant Manager initial that the section is complete, verifying that the trainee has attained the designated level of certification.

1. Lean Discipline Apprentice

	T	LMC	PM	Date	
A.	____	____	____	_____	Participate in a CI Overview Class
B.	____	____	____	_____	Participate in Lean Overview Training
C.	____	____	____	_____	Participate in 5S, STD Work, PPS, Error Proofing, QCO, and MM overview training

	T	LMC	PM	Date
Achieved Lean Discipline Apprentice Certification	_____	_____	_____	_____

2. Lean Discipline Generalist

	T	LMC	PM	Date	
A.	____	____	____	_____	Participate in a CI Train-the-Trainer class
B.	____	____	____	_____	Train and develop plant implementation team, plant leadership team, and shop-floor cell teams in a pilot area
C.	____	____	____	_____	Use 10-step CI methodologies to independently implement a major (5-day event) change in pilot area

Table 3.1 (continued)   LDE Checklist Document

2. Lean Discipline Generalist (continued)

	T	LMC	PM	Date	
D.	____	____	____	_____	Understand mission statement, strategies, and roles
E.	____	____	____	_____	Use data collection methods to highlight CI opportunities in a pilot area
F.	____	____	____	_____	Develop a plan for "Work" and "Equipment" CI events in designated pilot area
G.	____	____	____	_____	Achieve LDG in Standard Work
H.	____	____	____	_____	Achieve LDG in Process Problem Solving

	T	LMC	PM	Date
Achieved Lean Discipline Generalist Certification	____	_____	_____	_____

3. Lean Discipline Specialist

	T	LMC	PM	Date	
A.	____	____	____	_____	Document, analyze, and present results at the facility level to support CI events
B.	____	____	____	_____	Execute Breakout Schedule for CI events plantwide
C.	____	____	____	_____	Achieve LDG in TPM
D.	____	____	____	_____	Achieve LDG in QCO
E.	____	____	____	_____	Achieve LDG in Error Proofing
F.	____	____	____	_____	Use data collection methods to highlight CI opportunities plantwide
G.	____	____	____	_____	Develop a plan for "Work" and "Equipment" CI events plantwide
H.	____	____	____	_____	Perform regular audits on changes to confirm results

	T	LMC	PM	Date
Achieved Lean Discipline Specialist Certification	____	_____	_____	_____

continued

Table 3.1 (continued) LDE Checklist Document

4. **Lean Discipline Expert**					
	T	LMC	PM	Date	
A.	___	___	___	_____	Develop CI strategies, master schedule, and breakout schedules to support company goals and objectives
B.	___	___	___	_____	Use CI methodology to target and initiate activities for major areas for change
C.	___	___	___	_____	Develop log of all CI events for future use by company personnel across sites
D.	___	___	___	_____	Achieve LDG in MM
E.	___	___	___	_____	Set goals for Management/Shop-floor Team/CI Core Team and act as a resource for the core team
F.	___	___	___	_____	Share leadership of facility layouts, machinery equipment design, and process flow for new launches and production moves

				CORP	
	T	LMC	PM	Apprvl	Date
Achieved Lean Discipline Expert Certification	___	___	___	___	___

Those designated should be aware that there is more responsibility than just attaching their signature to a piece of paper when presented. The designees need to spend time with the LDE candidate and review any criteria that they are being asked to sign off on. This usually means taking some time to speak with the LDE candidate face to face, review the candidate's knowledge base, walk the Gemba with the candidate, and visually review any related work implemented. The designees will also want to ask questions of the LDE candidates to ensure that they are absorbing what they have learned and can apply the lessons, whether it be through classroom instruction or required reading materials. Only when satisfied that the LDE candidate fully comprehends the criteria should the designee sign off. Remember that these people ultimately will be your internal consultants for their related Lean discipline!

The documents I have provided are not protected and can be modified to fit your business needs. In the upper left-hand corner goes your company logo and the abbreviation of the name for your Lean management system. In the upper right corner is your Lean management system abbreviation (you will see this as XXX throughout the checklist documents) and the document control number. Additionally, the Human Resource manager or director should also sign as the approver of the checklist training document. "Why?" you may ask. Well, in my world, the Human Resource department is responsible for all training and training documentation. If you would like to designate a different person, you certainly could. The rest of the document is fairly self-explanatory, but again, if you need to change some of the verbiage to fit your needs, you have that ability.

At this same time, you should designate an owner to maintain the Lean Discipline Expert Status Look-Across Chart and the Required-Reading Look-Across Chart (see Figures 3.1 and 3.2). The Look-Across Charts are color-coded for each Lean discipline. The examples are only a sample of one section, a portion of a somewhat larger Excel spreadsheet, and I have hidden some rows from each so that you can get a better grasp of the charts.

Finally, the LDE Look-Across Chart should be owned and maintained by one individual and should be maintained electronically so that people may review it on a shared database, but it should be password protected so that the owner will be the only person authorized to make changes to the chart. Normally this is assigned to a representative in the Human Resource Department or to the Lean Manager.

The Lean Discipline Expert Status Look-Across Chart is basically a visual aid that clearly displays the progress or lack thereof for each Lean Discipline Champion and Lean Discipline Expert candidate. It also tracks progress for any required reading materials for Plant Management and the Lean Discipline Expert candidates as well.

I would suggest that this document be posted in the same room as your Lean library and be updated on a monthly basis prior to any scheduled review by the plant staff. The Lean Discipline Expert Look-Across Chart is a critical document that needs to be reviewed by the Staff at a minimum of a monthly basis. The Staff and Lean Champions need to monitor various Lean Discipline Candidates' progress and address any issues regarding lack of progress or roadblocks.

When a Lean Discipline Expert candidate is ready for the facilitation stage, it is important that the candidate feel as comfortable as possible

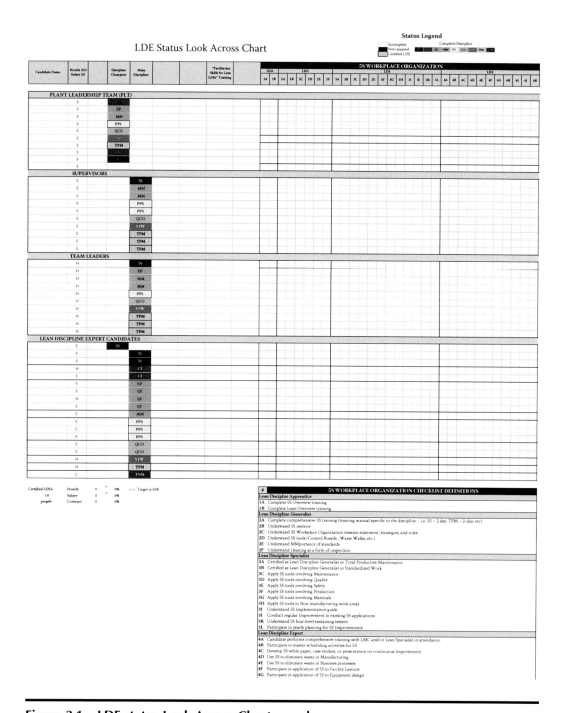

Figure 3.1 LDE status Look-Across Chart sample.

Plant Leadership Team & LDE Candidates Required Reading Material

CATEGORY	5S									CI			EP			
BOOK CODE	5S-1	5S-2	5S-3	5S-4	5S-5	5S-6	5S-7	5S-8	5S-9	CI-1	CI-2	CI-3	EP-1	EP-2	EP-3	EP-4
PLT MEMBERS																
LDE Candidates																

Lean Library Book Titles with Code

5S-1	5S for Operators: 5 Pillars of the Visual Workplace
5S-2	Visual Systems: Harnessing the Power of the Visual Workplace
5S-3	Who Moved My Cheese? An Amazing Way to Deal with Change in Your Work and in Your Life
5S-4	5S Challenges Video
5S-5	Kamishibai Boards A Lean Visual Management System That Supports Layered Audits
5S-6	5S for the Office
5S-7	Gemba Walks for Service Excellence
5S-8	Visual Controls, Applying Visual Management to the Factory Floor
5S-9	The 5S Pocket Guide

CI-1	Kaizen Revolution: How to Use Kaizen Events to Implement Lean Manufacturing and Improve Quality, Cost and Delivery
CI-2	Kaizen for the Shopfloor
CI-3	The Kaizen Blitz: Accelerating Breakthroughs in Productivity and Performance
CI-4	Progressive Kaizen the Key to Gaining a Global Competitive Edge
CI-5	The Kaizen Event Planner Achieving Rapid Improvement in the Office, Service & Technical Environment
CI-6	Kaizen the Art of Creative Thinking
CI-7	Kaizen the Key to Japan's Competitive Success

EP-1	Poka-Yoke: Improving Product Quality by Preventing Defects
EP-2	Zero Quality Control: Source Inspection and the Poka-Yoke System
EP-3	Mistake Proofing: Design Errors Out
EP-4	Mistake Proofing for Operators

Figure 3.2   Required reading Look-Across Chart sample.

presenting and training in a manner that conveys to the event that he/she is knowledgeable about their materials and can be recognized as the go-to person with questions or concerns.

The use of a feedback form at every training session, kaizen event, or any exercise that includes others is a helpful tool. Receiving an anonymous feedback form from everyone in attendance has always been a good way to keep me on my toes. It also made sure that I understood how well I was communicating with the people involved and what opportunities I had for improvement.

I remember very well, in my early days, handing out feedback forms at the end of a session, and my boss asked what I was doing. After I explained the purpose, he said, "That is quite risky, you know; you may get feedback you don't want to hear." I agreed that he was correct about the possibility of getting feedback I didn't want to hear, but I also shared with him, "How else am I supposed to get better if I don't receive some of that type of feedback?"

I encourage all Lean Discipline Expert candidates to use this form, or some adaptation, not only as they start to facilitate activities, but even later on. A typical feedback form is shown in Table 3.2. You will find all Feedback Forms for each Lean discipline under the downloads tab on the CRC Press website for the book http://www.crcpress.com/product/isbn/ 9781482253658

Finally, another must is deciding who will be signing the Award Certificate (Figure 3.3) for achieving Lean Discipline Expert status and what the actual reward will be for the candidate: one-time cash payment (how much), recognition ceremony (published or video distribution), a trophy (determine one design for use for all candidates), a combination of any of these thoughts, or something special you have thought of as a team. A person may become a Lean Discipline Expert in more than one Lean discipline, but the trophy and cash payment are generally only given once. However, you can decide what is best for your organization.

Remember, achieving Lean Discipline Expert status is a big deal! This has been not only a huge commitment by the company, but from the individuals themselves, and it should be treated as an important milestone in the candidate's career. Also, bear in mind that not all who attempt to achieve Lean Discipline Expert status will make it. Those who do not make the cut should not be made to feel less important to your organization. No matter how much they achieve, they can still help in making culture change and applying what they do know to your Lean journey.

Each Lean Discipline candidate is totally responsible for maintaining their original checklist, working with their supervisor or manager to schedule training, scheduling reviews for any required reading materials, ensuring that they acquire the appropriate signatures for areas of completion, making sure that they continually provide the Human Resource Department an updated copy for their personnel files, informing the owner of the Look-Across Chart to update their records to reflect the most recent activity, and monitoring the Look-Across Chart to ensure accuracy. Any Lean Champions who decide to go through the LDE process with their candidates would have the same responsibilities.

Table 3.2   LDE Facilitation Feedback Form

Course: *5S/Visual Management*   Participant Name (Optional): _____

Instructor(s): _____

Date: _____

Thank you for attending this class. Your opinions are important. Please take a few minutes to complete this survey. The information collected will be used to ensure the quality of this training program and to continuously improve it.

Course Objectives:

To what extent was each of the following course objectives met for you? Please check the box that best represents your opinion.

		Rating				
	Objective	*Fully met*	*Mostly met*	*Undecided*	*Somewhat met*	*Not met at all*
1.	Increased understanding of how 5S relates to the lean process					
2.	Increased ability to list the major reasons for implementing 5S/VM					
3.	Increased ability to identify the difference between normal and abnormal conditions					
4.	Increased ability to explain the basic components of visual factory					
5.	Increased ability to implement visual controls and displays in your workplace					

Comments: _____
_____

continued

Table 3.2 (continued)   LDE Facilitation Feedback Form

Course Materials:

Please rate the quality of the following items by checking the box that best represents your opinion.

		Rating				
	Item	*Very good*	*Good*	*Average*	*Poor*	*Very poor*
1.	Handouts					
2.	Overheads/slides					
3.	Exercises					

Comments: _____
_____

Course Delivery:

Please rate the effectiveness of the instructor(s) on the following items by checking the box that best represents your opinion.

		Rating				
	Item	*Very effective*	*Effective*	*Undecided*	*Ineffective*	*Very ineffective*
1.	Conveying the learning points of the Lean discipline					
2.	Encouraging participation					
3.	Balancing lecture and discussion					
4.	Giving clear direction for the exercises					
5.	Maintaining a helpful and friendly manner					
6.	Overall rating of this instructor(s)					

Comments: _____
_____

Table 3.2 (continued)   LDE Facilitation Feedback Form

Overall Course Evaluation:

Please rate the following items by checking the box that best represents your opinion.

	Item	Rating				
		Strongly agree	*Agree*	*Undecided/ neutral*	*Disagree*	*Strongly disagree*
1.	I am comfortable with the 5S/Visual Management terminology.					
2.	I am able to determine if and how 5S/Visual Management will improve my manufacturing process.					
3.	I am confident that I can assess the readiness of my manufacturing process for 5S/Visual Management and implement it.					

Comments: _____

_____

What, if anything, would prevent you from using 5S/Visual Management in your operation?_____

_____

Please note any additional comments about the course: _____

_____

Thank you!

The issuance of this Certificate is in recognition of	
[Insert Name]	
Outstanding Achievement and Demonstrated Leadership in becoming a:	
Certified Lean Discipline Expert (LDE)	
[Insert Discipline]	
Our drive for Continuous Improvement is never ending. Your expertise and job responsibilities will drive our Lean Initiatives as we eliminate waste, reduce variation and make improvements that guarantee our processes are robust.	
(Insert Name) CEO Company name	[Insert Name] Director Lean Implementation Company Name

Figure 3.3   Award Certificate Sample.

Chapter 4

LDE 5S/Visual Management

Taiichi Ohno, the father of the Toyota Production System, once said, and I am paraphrasing here, "If you cannot even implement and sustain 5S in your factory, how do you expect to be successful at any other Lean discipline?" Based on the source, I would say that 5S (Visual Management) is very important! Why else do you think that almost every House of Lean or Lean Pyramid you have ever seen has 5S/Visual Management as the foundation?

As you review the sections in the Lean Discipline Expert 5S checklist in Table 4.1 (5S LDE Apprentice, Generalist, Specialist, Expert), you may have some questions about the terminology I use, so I will attempt to anticipate them and respond accordingly for each section.

5S LDE Apprentice: Your Lean system should be able to provide an overview or general training on what 5S is and why it is important. Many Lean systems call this training *Lean 101* or *Introduction to Lean*. These are very general in nature and do not get into detailed specifics, but at the completion of training, the LDE Apprentice candidate is expected to understand how 5S, Workplace Organization, and Visual Management benefit the organization and how 5S integrates into Lean overall. The candidate should also have a basic understanding of an implementation approach, how activities are measured, and the metrics that are impacted. The 5S LDE candidate should start with some of the required reading materials.

5S LDE Generalist: In this section, the LDE candidate is getting into a deeper level of understanding of the what, where, when, why, and how of 5S. The candidate should now start to be able to recognize normal from abnormal conditions. Candidates in this section should also complete all the required reading materials from the Lean library to enhance their understanding and knowledge for the upcoming applications in the next level. At the Generalist level, we see the candidate applying the 5S tools and concepts in selected work areas as well as implementing the associated 5S metrics. The expectation as a Generalist is to train plant leadership, shop-floor groups, and others as needed and to develop plantwide 5S metrics and zone maps. The candidate should also know how to apply the Plan–Do–Check–Act (PDCA) tool to sustain those 5S elements that have been implemented.

5S LDE Specialist: At this level, the candidate will be getting into the details of 5S and coming up with ideas for the hands-on application of 5S. In the Specialist category for 5S, the LDE candidate also has to start getting into the cross functionality of Lean, particularly Total Productive Maintenance and Standard Work. If you have read the Preface to this book, you may remember that I mentioned that Lean disciplines are meant to interact and are not stand-alone disciplines. The plant is starting to take advantage of the knowledge of the 5S LDE candidate by applying 5S directly to Maintenance, Quality, Safety, Production, Scheduling, and Materials. The candidate will analyze, based upon the available documentation, the results of the 5S activities to the plant-level management team and develop a plan for plantwide implementation of 5S. At the Specialist level, the candidate will also implement the means of sustaining 5S activities, including PDCA walks, and may or may not also be exposed to some difficulty in maintaining what has been gained. This is usually determined by the level of Lean culture in the plant. Either way, these are good lessons for the 5S LDE candidate to learn. If it was easy, anybody could do it! I think we have all learned that lesson.

5S LDE Expert: A candidate's leadership and training skills should be evident at the Expert level, along with an ability to document and present results to any group at the plant or corporate levels. At this level, it is important for candidates to be able to develop plans, strategies, and objectives to use their Lean discipline to eliminate waste not only in manufacturing, but at the business level, too! At the Expert level, the LDE candidate is not only contributing to the plant in many areas, but is also getting involved with other plant teams such as Engineering, Production Control & Logistics, and Purchasing on how the 5S tools can be applied at the *beginning* of those departments' processes, rather than after the fact. At this level, the candidate should be a valuable resource to the plant or company in all aspects of the 5S application.

Once the 5S LDE candidate begins facilitating training or events, it is very important that the candidate receive feedback not only on their performance and knowledge of the materials, but the materials themselves. Table 4.2 is an example of a good LDE Facilitation Feedback Form. If you feel that any modification is needed to improve the form, please feel free to do so. All forms are on located under the downloads tab on the CRC Press website for the book http://www.crcpress.com/product/isbn/9781482253658

Table 4.1   5S Lean Discipline Expert Checklist

Your Company Logo Here	Your Lean System Initials Here	Title: Training Overview Checklist for 5S LDEs	Date: August 15, 2014	Rev: 1.0	Page: Page 1 of 3	Document No.: XXX-5S-7001 Approved by: HR Manager

Starting Date: ____/____/____   Trainee's Name:_____
(Please Print Legibly)

Training Overview Checklist for 5S LDEs

This training checklist is to be utilized in training 5S LDEs. Each item needs to be covered by the support personnel listed. As the trainee completes an item, the trainee (T) initials and dates the item. The Lean Manager/Coordinator (LMC) and Plant Manager (PM) initial to indicate the training is completed.

When a section is completed, the trainee, the Lean Manager/Coordinator, and the Plant Manager initial that the section is complete, verifying that the trainee has attained the designated level of certification.

1. Lean Discipline Apprentice

	T	LMC	PM	Date	
A.	____	____	____	_____	Participate in 5S Overview Class
B.	____	____	____	_____	Participate in Lean Overview Training

		T	LMC	PM	Date
Achieved Lean Discipline Apprentice Certification		_____	_____	_____	_____

2. Lean Discipline Generalist

	T	LMC	PM	Date	
A.	____	____	____	_____	Participate in 5S Train-the-Trainer training class
B.	____	____	____	_____	Understand 5S metrics
C.	____	____	____	_____	Understand mission statement, strategies, and roles
D.	____	____	____	_____	Understand 5S tools (Kamishibai Boards, Waste Walks, etc.)

Table 4.1 (continued)   5S Lean Discipline Expert Checklist

	T	LMC	PM	Date	
2. Lean Discipline Generalist (continued)					
E.	___	___	___	_____	Understand importance of standards
F.	___	___	___	_____	Understand cleaning as a form of inspection

	T	LMC	PM	Date
Achieved Lean Discipline Generalist Certification	___	___	___	___

	T	LMC	PM	Date	
3. Lean Discipline Specialist					
A.	___	___	___	_____	Apply 5S tools in the following areas: • Maintenance
B.	___	___	___	_____	• Quality
C.	___	___	___	_____	• Safety
D.	___	___	___	_____	• Production
E.	___	___	___	_____	• Materials
F.	___	___	___	_____	• Non-production areas
G.	___	___	___	_____	Understand 5S implementation guide
H.	___	___	___	_____	Obtain Lean Discipline Generalist in: • Total Productive Maintenance
I.	___	___	___	_____	• Standard Work
J.	___	___	___	_____	Conduct regular PDCA to existing 5S installations
K.	___	___	___	_____	Understand 5S four-level sustaining system
L.	___	___	___	_____	Participate in yearly planning for 5S improvements

	T	LMC	PM	Date
Achieved Lean Discipline Specialist Certification	___	___	___	___

continued

Table 4.1 (continued)   5S Lean Discipline Expert Checklist

4. Lean Discipline Expert					
	T	LMC	PM	Date	
A.	___	___	___	_____	Participate in master scheduling activities for 5S
B.	___	___	___	_____	Develop 5S white paper, case studies, or presentation on continuous improvement
					Use 5S to eliminate waste in the following areas:
C.	___	___	___	_____	• Manufacturing
D.	___	___	___	_____	• Business
					Participate in application of 5S to:
E.	___	___	___	_____	• Facility layouts
F.	___	___	___	_____	• Equipment design
G.	___	___	___	_____	• Process flow
H.	___	___	___	_____	Recognized as 5S resource to plant
I.	___	___	___	_____	Understand 5S standards for new equipment and work areas

	T	LMC	PM	CORP Apprvl	Date
Achieved Lean Discipline Expert Certification	___	___	___	___	___

Table 4.2 LDE Facilitation Feedback Form

Course: *5S/Visual Management*   Participant Name (Optional): _____

Instructor(s): _____

Date: _____

Thank you for attending this class. Your opinions are important. Please take a few minutes to complete this survey. The information collected will be used to ensure the quality of this training program and to continuously improve it.

Course Objectives:

To what extent was each of the following course objectives met for you? Please check the box that best represents your opinion.

	Objective	Fully met	Mostly met	Undecided	Somewhat met	Not met at all
		Rating				
1.	Increased understanding of how 5S relates to the Lean process					
2.	Increased ability to list the major reasons for implementing 5S/VM					
3.	Increased ability to identify the difference between normal and abnormal conditions					
4.	Increased ability to explain the basic components of visual factory					
5.	Increased ability to implement visual controls and displays in your workplace					

Comments: _____
_____

continued

Table 4.2 (continued)   LDE Facilitation Feedback Form

Course Materials:

Please rate the quality of the following items by checking the box that best represents your opinion.

		Rating				
	Item	*Very good*	*Good*	*Average*	*Poor*	*Very poor*
1.	Handouts					
2.	Overheads/slides					
3.	Exercises					

Comments: _____

_____

Course Delivery:

Please rate the effectiveness of the instructor(s) on the following items by checking the box that best represents your opinion.

		Rating				
	Item	*Very effective*	*Effective*	*Undecided*	*Ineffective*	*Very ineffective*
1.	Conveying the learning points of the subject matter					
2.	Encouraging participation					
3.	Balancing lecture and discussion					
4.	Giving clear direction for the exercises					
5.	Maintaining a helpful and friendly manner					
6.	Overall rating of this instructor(s)					

Comments: _____

_____

Table 4.2 (continued)   LDE Facilitation Feedback Form

Overall Course Evaluation:

Please rate the following items by checking the box that best represents your opinion.

	Item	Rating				
		Strongly agree	*Agree*	*Undecided/ neutral*	*Disagree*	*Strongly disagree*
1.	I am comfortable with the 5S/Visual Management terminology.					
2.	I am able to determine if and how 5S/Visual Management will improve my manufacturing process.					
3.	I am confident that I can assess the readiness of my manufacturing process for 5S/Visual Management and implement it.					

Comments: _____

_____

What, if anything, would prevent you from using 5S/Visual Management in your operation?_____

_____

Please note any additional comments about the course: _____

_____

Thank you!

Chapter 5

LDE Value Stream Mapping

As you review the Value Stream Mapping LDE checklist (Table 5.1), there are two characteristics that I think are critical attributes for your Value Stream Mapping Lean Discipline Expert candidate:

1. A person who can envision the "big picture" or what the future may look like if you do this or that
2. A person with very good eyes for waste and flow

I believe these to be critical attributes because the Value Stream Map is your battle plan for attacking waste and non-value-added items such as safety, inventory, motion, people, quality, equipment, and standard work in a single value stream, plant value stream, or an enterprise value stream.

The Value Stream Mapping LDE candidate is going have to be able to teach others to see the non-value-added waste in any value stream, identify all levels of opportunities to add value for the Customer, and create the vision for the future state based on eliminating the non-value-added wastes identified. The Value Stream Mapping candidate needs to have the ability to draw all this out in the language of Value Stream Maps (the icons), communicate what it all means, and show the methodology for calculating the impact of cost versus savings not only to the people in the value stream exercise, but to top-level management.

Since the Value Stream Mapping LDE candidate will be responsible for teaching Value Stream Mapping and Waste Walk training and identification, I have included examples of course feedback forms (Tables 5.2 and 5.3) for

Table 5.1   Value Stream Mapping Lean Discipline Expert Checklist

Your Company Logo Here	Your Lean System Initials Here	Title: Training Overview Checklist for *VSM* LDEs	Date: August 21, 2014	Rev: 1.0	Page: Page 1 of 1	Document No.: XXX-VSM-7002 Approved by: HR Manager

Starting Date: ___/___/___   Trainee's Name:_____

(Please Print Legibly)

Training Overview Checklist for VSM LDEs

This training checklist is to be utilized in training Value Stream Mapping LDEs. Each item needs to be covered by the support personnel listed. As the trainee completes an item, the trainee (T) initials and dates the item. The Lean Manager/Coordinator (LMC) and Plant Manager (PM) initial to indicate that the training is completed.

When a section is completed, the trainee, the Lean Manager/Coordinator, and the Plant Manager initial that the section is complete, verifying that the trainee has attained the designated level of certification.

1. Lean Discipline Apprentice

	T	LMC	PM	Date	
A.	___	___	___	_____	Participate in a VSM Overview Class and a Waste Class including a Waste Walk Exercise
B.	___	___	___	_____	Participate in Lean, Material Management, and Standard Work Overview Training

	T	LMC	PM	Date
Achieved Lean Discipline Apprentice Certification	_____	_____	_____	_____

2. Lean Discipline Generalist

	T	LMC	PM	Date	
A.	___	___	___	_____	Participate in a VSM event where a Current State and Future State map is developed
B.	___	___	___	_____	Train and develop plant implementation team, plant leadership team, and shop-floor cell teams in a pilot area, not in Value Stream Mapping but Waste Training, and conduct a Waste Walk exercise

Table 5.1 (continued)   Value Stream Mapping Lean Discipline Expert Checklist

2. <u>Lean Discipline Generalist</u> (continued)

	T	LMC	PM	Date	
C.	____	____	____	_____	Achieve LDG in MM
D.	____	____	____	_____	Understand mission statement, strategies, and roles
E.	____	____	____	_____	Collect data in pilot area to help prioritize which opportunities to focus on
F.	____	____	____	_____	Participate in VSM Train-the-Trianer class

	T LMC PM Date
Achieved Lean Discipline Generalist Certification	____ ____ ____ ____

3. <u>Lean Discipline Specialist</u>

	T	LMC	PM	Date	
A.	____	____	____	_____	Document, analyze, and present results at the facility level to support VSM events
B.	____	____	____	_____	Execute Master Schedule for implementing VSM events plantwide
C.	____	____	____	_____	Achieve LDG in Standard Work
D.	____	____	____	_____	Use data collection methods to highlight VSM opportunities plantwide
E.	____	____	____	_____	Perform regular audits on changes to confirm results

	T LMC PM Date
Achieved Lean Discipline Specialist Certification	____ ____ ____ ____

4. <u>Lean Discipline Expert</u>

	T	LMC	PM	Date	
A.	____	____	____	_____	Develop VSM strategies, master schedule, and breakout schedules to support company goals and objectives
B.	____	____	____	_____	Use VSM methodology to target and initiate activities for areas for major change

continued

Table 5.1 (continued)   Value Stream Mapping Lean Discipline Expert Checklist

4. Lean Discipline Expert (continued)					
	T	LMC	PM	Date	
C.	___	___	___	_____	Develop log of all VSM events for future use by company personnel across sites
D.	___	___	___	_____	Set goals for management/shop-floor team/VSM Core Team and act as a resource for the core team
E.	___	___	___	_____	Share leadership of facility layouts, machinery equipment design, and process flow for new launches and production moves

				CORP	
	T	LMC	PM	Apprvl	Date
Achieved Lean Discipline Expert Certification	___	___	___	___	___

both of these in this chapter as well as on the CRC Press website at http://www.crcpress.com/product/isbn/9781482253658.

Value Stream Mapping LDE Apprentice: To complete the basic understanding portion, the candidate will need to be exposed to not only Lean and Value Stream Mapping overviews, but Waste, Inventory Management, and Standard Work as well. These multiple subjects cross over heavily into Current State as well as Future State Value Stream Maps.

The candidate should begin to read the required reading materials, especially *Learning to See* (Rother and Shook) to gain an understanding of the Value Stream Map icon language and analysis tools, how to measure and explain the opportunities identified, how to apply that to the business metrics, how to develop an implementation approach, how to explain the potential benefits to the plant, and how Value Stream Mapping and Waste identification incorporate with all other Lean activities.

Value Stream Mapping LDE Generalist: During this section, the candidates will have completed extensive Value Stream Mapping training and continue to educate themselves through the required reading materials. The LDE candidate, as a Generalist, will apply Value Stream Mapping concepts, tools, and baseline metrics; will participate in the development of Current and Future State Value Stream Maps; apply data collection and analysis; and train and develop associates at all levels in creating Value Stream Maps and Waste identification. As a Value Stream Mapping LDE Generalist, the candidate will also be able to implement Mapping with assistance from internal or external resources.

Value Stream Mapping LDE Specialist: At this stage, the Value Stream Mapping LDE candidate will have achieved the status of being a Generalist in Material Management and Standard Work. The candidate should be relating to the senior plant-level management, documenting and analyzing all Value Stream Mapping activities taking place in the facility, identifying additional opportunities plantwide for areas to be Value Stream Mapped, and developing the implementation plan for plantwide Value Stream Mapping and training. At this point, the Value Stream LDE candidate also should begin leading all Value Stream Mapping activities throughout the plant, be responsible for recording the improvement in plant metrics as it relates to the Value Stream Mapping activities, showing the ability to lead implementation and sustainment efforts, and have a very in-depth understanding of the relationship between Lean tools and how they support the company's vision, goals, and objectives. Upon completion of this stage, all required reading materials should have been completed.

Value Stream Mapping LDE Expert: At the LDE Expert level, the candidate should be developing excellent public speaking skills, as they are teaching, coaching, mentoring associates, and leading the Value Stream Mapping improvements and best practices identified during the mapping process. The Value Stream Mapping candidate should be heavily involved with other departments with regard to facility layouts, cell layouts, new machinery, equipment design, and process flows throughout the facility. Additionally, the candidate should be able to share the plant's long-term vision of plant layouts, processes, and new business potentials.

Table 5.2   LDE Facilitation Feedback Form

Course: *Value Stream Mapping*   Participant Name (Optional): _____

Instructor(s): _____

Date: _____

Thank you for attending this class. Your opinions are important to us. Please take a few minutes to complete this survey. The information collected will be used to ensure the quality of this training program and to continuously improve it.

Course Objectives:

To what extent was each of the following course objectives met for you? Please check the box that best represents your opinion.

	Objective	Rating				
		Fully met	*Mostly met*	*Undecided*	*Somewhat met*	*Not met at all*
1.	Increased understanding of what the Value Stream Mapping is					
2.	Increased ability to understand Flow and identify opportunities					
3.	Increased ability to create Current and Future State Maps					
4.	Increased skill in identifying tools to use for continuous improvement					

Comments: _____
_____

Table 5.2 (continued)   LDE Facilitation Feedback Form

Course Materials:

Please rate the quality of the following items by checking the box that best represents your opinion.

		Rating				
	Item	Very good	Good	Average	Poor	Very poor
1.	Handouts					
2.	Overheads/Slides					
3.	Exercises					

Comments: _____
_____

Course Delivery:

Please rate the effectiveness of the instructor(s) on the following items by checking the box that best represents your opinion.

		Rating				
	Item	Very effective	Effective	Undecided	Ineffective	Very ineffective
1.	Conveying the learning points of the subject matter					
2.	Encouraging participation					
3.	Balancing lecture and discussion					
4.	Giving clear direction for the exercises					
5.	Maintaining a helpful and friendly manner					
6.	Overall rating of this instructor(s)					

Comments: _____
_____

continued

Table 5.2 (continued)   LDE Facilitation Feedback Form

Overall Course Evaluation:

Please rate the following items using by checking the box that best represents your opinion.

		Rating				
	Item	Strongly agree	Agree	Undecided/ neutral	Disagree	Strongly disagree
1.	I have a better understanding of the importance of using Value Stream Maps for improvement.					
2.	I believe that Value Stream Mapping is an important tool.					
3.	I am confident that Continuous Improvements can be successfully implemented in my process/job.					

Comments: _____

_____

What, if anything, would prevent you from successfully using this tool? _____

_____

Please note any additional comments about the course: _____

_____

Thank you!

Table 5.3   LDE Facilitation Feedback Form

Course: Waste Training & Waste Walk   Participant Name (Optional): _____

Instructor(s): _____

Date: _____

Thank you for attending this class. Your opinions are important to us. Please take a few minutes to complete this survey. The information collected will be used to ensure the quality of this training program and to continuously improve it.

Course Objectives:

To what extent was each of the following course objectives met for you? Please check the box that best represents your opinion.

	Objective	Rating				
		Fully met	*Mostly met*	*Undecided*	*Somewhat met*	*Not met at all*
1.	Increased understanding of what the 7 Forms of Waste are					
2.	Increased ability to understand the 7 Forms of Waste					
3.	Increased ability to recognize the 7 Forms of Waste					
4.	Increased skill in identifying tools to use to eliminate the 7 Forms of Waste					

Comments: _____
_____

continued

Table 5.3 (continued)   LDE Facilitation Feedback Form

Course Materials:

Please rate the quality of the following items by checking the box that best represents your opinion.

	Item	Rating				
		Very good	*Good*	*Average*	*Poor*	*Very poor*
1.	Handouts					
2.	Overheads/Slides					
3.	Exercises					

Comments: _____
_____

Course Delivery:

Please rate the effectiveness of the instructor(s) on the following items by checking the box that best represents your opinion.

	Item	Rating				
		Very effective	*Effective*	*Undecided*	*Ineffective*	*Very ineffective*
1.	Conveying the learning points of the subject matter					
2.	Encouraging participation					
3.	Balancing lecture and discussion					
4.	Giving clear direction for the exercises					
5.	Maintaining a helpful and friendly manner					
6.	Overall rating of this instructor(s)					

Comments: _____
_____

Table 5.3 (continued)   LDE Facilitation Feedback Form

Overall Course Evaluation: Please rate the following items by checking the box that best represents your opinion.						
				Rating		
	Item	*Strongly agree*	*Agree*	*Undecided/ neutral*	*Disagree*	*Strongly disagree*
1.	I have a better understanding of the importance of recognizing the 7 Forms of Waste in a Lean System.					
2.	I believe that eliminating Waste will improve my process/job.					
3.	I am confident that Waste elimination can be successfully implemented in my process/job.					

Comments: _____
_____

What, if anything, would prevent you from eliminating Waste on your job? _____
_____

Please note any additional comments about the course: _____
_____

Thank you!

Chapter 6

LDE Standard Work (Cyclical and Noncyclical)

When Standard Work is applied correctly, it generously complements all other Lean disciplines! Cyclical and noncyclical Standard Work both have a huge impact on safety, repeatability, quality, and productivity as well.

Cyclical Standard Work applies to associates who perform the same sequence of tasks each and every cycle. For example, as an associate working in an assembly cell, I was required to place a machined cast-iron piece into a moving fixture and then place a rubber grommet around the neck of the machine's casting. This occurred every time, every cycle of the machine. The time allotted for this activity was 6 seconds. I have seen cyclical cycle times as long as 12 minutes. Cyclical Standard Work can also occur in business processes. For example, as an associate working in the Purchasing Department, I was required to enter new and renewed purchase orders into the company's computer system. I performed this work all day, and it was all I did.

Noncyclical Standard Work applies to associates who may or may not perform the same task throughout the workday, but not every cycle. For example, a Quality Auditor's work may consist of going to different processes throughout the day and making quality checks at various stages of those processes to ensure that a quality product was being produced. Noncyclical Standard Work occurs frequently in business processes, as many associates working in the office environment complete multiple tasks throughout their workday. For example, as an associate working in the Engineering Department, I may start my workday working on machine design, then working with machines suppliers, then writing machine quotes, etc. As you can see, I am not performing the same task every cycle. If you take the time to look around your work environment, there are many examples of cyclical and noncyclical Standard Work both in manufacturing and business processes.

There are also different tools used in creating cyclical and noncyclical Standard Work. For example, with cyclical Standard Work, you will use a time-measurement sheet that gathers the work sequence time data on 10 complete cycles of an associate's work. When you are collecting data on a noncyclical activity, the Yamazumi chart is used due to the fact that the associate is not performing the exact same task every cycle, and data collection takes place for the entire shift.

For all of the above reasons, it is the intent of the Lean Discipline Expert process to have cyclical Standard Work and noncyclical Standard Work as two separate and distinct LDE categories! I highly recommend that the LDE candidate complete all the requirements for Cyclical Lean Discipline Expert *before* going to the requirements for Noncyclical Lean Discipline Expert. Otherwise, based on my experience, they will become frustrated, lost, and usually quit. I can think of only one circumstance where it would not be a requirement to become a Lean Discipline Expert in Cyclical Standard Work before signing up for the Lean Discipline Expert Noncyclical Standard Work category. That circumstance would be an Industrial Engineer who was trained in cyclical Standard Work application in college, but even those with such training may find it useful to become a Lean Discipline Expert in Cyclical Standard Work first. By no means would I suggest a LDE candidate to attempt both at the same time.

As you will see as you review the criteria for both Cyclical and Noncyclical Lean Discipline Experts, the goals to complete are basically the same, but the tools used to accomplish those goals will be different.

Standard Work LDE Apprentice: In the Apprentice section (Cyclical Table 6.1; Noncyclical Table 6.2), the candidate receives a basic exposure to Standard Work, 5S, Value Stream Mapping, and general Lean application. The expectation at the end of this section is that the LDE candidate will understand how and why Standard Work integrates and complements the total Lean journey. Additionally, the Lean Discipline Expert candidate should by now understand how Standard Work benefits the company, how the activity is measured, and what business metrics are affected. They should have developed an implementation approach they can work with. The candidate should also start to read the required reading material list on the LDE Look-Across Chart.

Standard Work LDE Generalist: The Standard Work LDE needs exposure to and understanding of the Company vision, strategies, and roles expected for Standard Work application, and many times this comes right from the Value Stream Map. As a LDE Generalist, the candidate will complete comprehensive Standard Work training through a combination of required reading materials, classroom interaction, and hands-on application in limited areas. The Standard Work LDE will also establish and implement Standard Work baseline metrics and, with assistance, begin to train associates at all levels in Standard Work to include calculating value-added labor percentages, floor space, and capital investment. At the completion of the Standard Work training, the LDE Generalist will totally grasp and understand Takt* application and calculations, processes reliability and repeatability, and how these impact quality metrics for an area.

Standard Work LDE Specialist: I personally believe that there is no better education than hands-on application, and as you can see in the Standard Work LDE Specialist category, that is what the candidate will receive a lot of! Not only does the LDE candidate apply the tools they have learned, they also need to sustain their implementation. The best way I know how to do this is to implement an audit process to constantly monitor whether associates are maintaining the standards put into place.

Under no circumstances should associates change or modify a standard in any way without consulting with the Standard Work Lean Discipline Expert candidate. Now that does not mean that the associates have no input into the standard developed, because they are an integral part of the development process. The Standard Work LDE should already realize this and should have developed a positive working relationship with associates in any area where the candidate is making Standard Work applications.

As a Standard Work LDE Specialist, the candidate will have developed a manual for the company on how to go about implementing

---

* Takt is calculated dividing available seconds per day by the Customer demand per day. This gives you how often you need to generate product for the Customer.

Standard Work, and be able to document and analyze data and metric performance, areas of challenge, and sustainment results. The candidate should be comfortable in reporting anything related to Standard Work, as well as their progress or roadblocks, to the plant staff individually or as a group. The Standard Work LDE candidate should always use Tables 6.3 (Cyclical Standard Work) or 6.4 (Noncyclical Standard Work) whenever facilitating training so they can understand how others perceive them and their communication skills. This is an opportunity for continuous improvement for the candidate.

Based upon the training experiences, the candidate should also work with the Human Resource Department to refine the training methods for this subject, providing suggestions for any type of modification that could help strengthen the development of Standard Work LDE candidates. The plant should be seeing this candidate as the go-to person for anything related to Standard Work. The LDE candidate should be able to really have a vision as to how Standard Work interacts with other Lean tools and potentially see areas of application that have been previously overlooked. All of the required reading materials should be completed at by the end of the LDE Specialist section.

Standard Work LDE Expert: At this point, the Standard Work LDE candidate is really being drawn into a leadership role. The LDE candidate is being called upon by the plant staff to apply their knowledge to areas such as equipment design, layout design, machinery positioning, and process flows. The LDE candidate should be documenting best practices so that the proverbial "wheel" does not have to be reinvented, expanding the company vision of Standard Work applications, and exceeding company goals on a regular basis when applying Standard Work techniques.

Table 6.1   Cyclical Standard Work Lean Discipline Expert Checklist

Your Company Logo Here	Your Lean System Initials Here	**Title:** *Training Overview Checklist for Cyclical Standard Work LDEs*	**Date:** August 21, 2014	**Rev:** 1.0	**Page:** Page 1 of 1	**Document No.:** XXX-SW-7003 **Approved by:** HR Manager

Starting Date: ____/____/____   Trainee's Name:_____

(Please Print Legibly)

Training Overview Checklist for Cyclical Standard Work LDEs

This training checklist is to be utilized in training Cyclical Standard Work LDEs. Each item needs to be covered by the support personnel listed. As the trainee completes an item, the trainee (T) initials and dates the item. The Lean Manager/Coordinator (LMC) and Plant Manager (PM) initial to indicate that the training is completed.

When a section is completed, the trainee, the Lean Manager/Coordinator, and the Plant Manager initial that the section is complete, verifying that the trainee has attained the designated level of certification.

1. Lean Discipline Apprentice

	T	LMC	PM	Date	
A.	____	____	____	_____	Participate in Cyclical Standard Work Overview Class
B.	____	____	____	_____	Participate in Lean Overview Training
C.	____	____	____	_____	Complete 5S Training

	T	LMC	PM	Date
Achieved Lean Discipline Apprentice Certification	_____	_____	_____	_____

2. Lean Discipline Generalist

	T	LMC	PM	Date	
A.	____	____	____	_____	Establish and implement Cyclical STW metrics to establish a pilot area baseline
B.	____	____	____	_____	Understand Cyclical STW mission statement, strategy, and roles
C.	____	____	____	_____	Improve operator efficiency in a pilot area

	T	LMC	PM	Date
Achieved Lean Discipline Generalist Certification	_____	_____	_____	_____

continued

Table 6.1 (continued)   Cyclical Standard Work Lean Discipline Expert Checklist

	T	LMC	PM	Date	
3. Lean Discipline Specialist					
A.	___	___	___	_____	Apply Cyclical Standard Work tools in the following areas: • Maintenance
B.	___	___	___	_____	• Quality
C.	___	___	___	_____	• Safety
D.	___	___	___	_____	• Production
E.	___	___	___	_____	• Scheduling
F.	___	___	___	_____	• Materials
G.	___	___	___	_____	Execute breakout schedule for Standard Work implementation for a plant area
H.	___	___	___	_____	Achieve Generalist certification in 5S
I.	___	___	___	_____	Conduct regular PDCA on all areas where Cyclical STW has been implemented
J.	___	___	___	_____	Define cross-training/rotation pattern for Cyclical STW
K.	___	___	___	_____	Participate in Standard Work Train-the-Trainer class
L.	___	___	___	_____	Teach Cyclical Standard Work Overview class

	T	LMC	PM	Date
Achieved Lean Discipline Specialist Certification	_____	_____	_____	_____

	T	LMC	PM	Date	
4. Lean Discipline Expert					
A.	___	___	___	_____	Participate in annual planning for continuous improvement of Standard Work
B.	___	___	___	_____	Apply Six Sigma tools to address variation in Standard Work
C.	___	___	___	_____	Participate in goal setting for plant and corporate teams

Table 6.1 (continued)   Cyclical Standard Work Lean Discipline Expert Checklist

4. Lean Discipline Expert (continued)					
	T	**LMC**	**PM**	**Date**	
D.	____	____	____	_____	Participate in the following activities: • New facility layout or modification to existing layout
E.	____	____	____	_____	• Equipment design or modification
F.	____	____	____	_____	• Process flow design or modification
G.	____	____	____	_____	Participate in goal setting for management/ shop-floor teams
H.	____	____	____	_____	Recognized as a resource for management/ shop-floor teams
I.	____	____	____	_____	Achieve Generalist certification for Process Problem Solving (PPS)

			CORP	
T	**LMC**	**PM**	**Apprvl**	**Date**

Achieved Lean Discipline Expert Certification   ____ ____ ____ ____ ____

Table 6.2   Noncyclical Standard Work Lean Discipline Expert Checklist

Your Company Logo Here	Your Lean System Initials Here	Title: *Training Overview Checklist for Noncyclical Standard Work LDEs*	Date: August 21, 2014	Rev: 1.0	Page: Page 1 of 1	Document No.: XXX-SW-7004 Approved by: HR Manager

Starting Date: ____/____/____   Trainee's Name:_____

                                                                 (Please Print Legibly)

Training Overview Checklist for Noncyclical Standard Work LDEs

This training checklist is to be utilized in training Noncyclical Standard Work LDEs. Each item needs to be covered by the support personnel listed. As the trainee completes an item, the trainee (T) initials and dates the item. The Lean Manager/Coordinator (LMC) and Plant Manager (PM) initial to indicate that the training is completed.

When a section is completed the trainee, the Lean Manager/Coordinator, and the Plant Manager initial that the section is complete, verifying that the trainee has attained the designated level of certification.

5. Lean Discipline Apprentice

	T	LMC	PM	Date	
A.	____	____	____	_____	Participate in Noncyclical Standard Work Overview Class
B.	____	____	____	_____	Participate in Lean Overview Training
C.	____	____	____	_____	Complete 5S Training

	T	LMC	PM	Date
Achieved Lean Discipline Apprentice Certification	_____	_____	_____	_____

Table 6.2 (continued)   Noncyclical Standard Work Lean Discipline Expert Checklist

6. Lean Discipline Generalist					
	T	LMC	PM	Date	
A.	____	____	____	_____	Establish and implement Noncyclical STW metrics to establish a pilot area baseline
B.	____	____	____	_____	Understand Noncyclical STW mission statement, strategy, and roles
C.	____	____	____	_____	Improve operator efficiency in a pilot area

		T	LMC	PM	Date
Achieved Lean Discipline Generalist Certification		____	____	____	____

7. Lean Discipline Specialist					
	T	LMC	PM	Date	
A.	____	____	____	_____	Apply Noncyclical Standard Work tools in the following areas: • Maintenance
B.	____	____	____	_____	• Quality
C.	____	____	____	_____	• Safety
D.	____	____	____	_____	• Production
E.	____	____	____	_____	• Scheduling
F.	____	____	____	_____	• Materials
G.	____	____	____	_____	Execute breakout schedule for Standard Work implementation for a plant area
H.	____	____	____	_____	Achieve generalist certification in 5S
I.	____	____	____	_____	Conduct regular PDCA on all areas where STW has been implemented
J.	____	____	____	_____	Define cross-training/rotation pattern for Noncyclical STW

continued

Table 6.2 (continued)   Noncyclical Standard Work Lean Discipline Expert Checklist

7. **Lean Discipline Specialist** (continued)					
	T	**LMC**	**PM**	**Date**	
K.	___	___	___	_____	Participate in Noncyclical Standard Work Train-the-Trainer class
L.	___	___	___	_____	Teach Noncyclical Standard Work Overview class

	T	**LMC**	**PM**	**Date**
Achieved Lean Discipline Specialist Certification	_____	_____	_____	_____

8. **Lean Discipline Expert**					
	T	**LMC**	**PM**	**Date**	
A.	___	___	___	_____	Participate in annual planning for continuous improvement of Noncyclical Standard Work
B.	___	___	___	_____	Apply Six Sigma tools to address variation in Standard Work
C.	___	___	___	_____	Participate in goal setting for plant and corporate teams
					Participate in the following activities:
D.	___	___	___	_____	• New facility layout or modification to existing layout
E.	___	___	___	_____	• Equipment design or modification
F.	___	___	___	_____	• Process flow design or modification
G.	___	___	___	_____	Participate in goal setting for management/ shop-floor teams
H.	___	___	___	_____	Recognized as a resource for management/ shop-floor teams
I.	___	___	___	_____	Achieve Generalist certification for Process Problem Solving (PPS)

	T	**LMC**	**PM**	**CORP Apprvl**	**Date**
Achieved Lean Discipline Expert Certification	_____	_____	_____	_____	_____

Table 6.3   LDE Facilitation Feedback Form

Course: *Cyclical Standard Work*   Participant Name (Optional): _____

Instructor(s): _____

Date: _____

Thank you for attending this class. Your opinions are important to us. Please take a few minutes to complete this survey. The information collected will be used to ensure the quality of this training program and to continuously improve it.

Course Objectives:

To what extent was each of the following course objectives met for you? Please check the box that best represents your opinion.

		Rating				
	Objective	*Fully met*	*Mostly met*	*Undecided*	*Somewhat met*	*Not met at all*
1.	Increased understanding of what Cyclical Standard Work is					
2.	Increased ability to develop a case for using Cyclical Standard Work					
3.	Increased ability to recognize Cyclical Standard Work					
4.	Increased skill in identifying barriers to Cyclical Standard Work and ways to overcome them using Cyclical Standard Work tools					

Comments: _____
_____

continued

Table 6.3 (continued)   LDE Facilitation Feedback Form

Course Materials:

Please rate the quality of the following items by checking the box that best represents your opinion.

		Rating				
	Item	Very good	Good	Average	Poor	Very poor
1.	Handouts					
2.	Overheads/Slides					
3.	Exercises					

Comments: _____

_____

Course Delivery:

Please rate the effectiveness of the instructor(s) on the following items by checking the box that best represents your opinion.

		Rating				
	Item	Very effective	Effective	Undecided	Ineffective	Very ineffective
1.	Conveying the learning points of the Lean Discipline					
2.	Encouraging participation					
3.	Balancing lecture and discussion					
4.	Giving clear direction for the exercises					
5.	Maintaining a helpful and friendly manner					
6.	Overall rating of this instructor(s)					

Comments: _____

_____

Table 6.3 (continued)   LDE Facilitation Feedback Form

Overall Course Evaluation:

Please rate the following items by checking the box that best represents your opinion.

	Item	Rating				
		Strongly agree	*Agree*	*Undecided/ neutral*	*Disagree*	*Strongly disagree*
1.	I have a better understanding of the importance of Cyclical Standard Work in a Lean System.					
2.	I believe that Cyclical Standard Work will improve my process/job.					
3.	I am confident that Cyclical Standard Work can be successfully implemented in my process/job.					

Comments: _____

_____

What, if anything, would prevent you from using Cyclical Standard Work on your job?_____

_____

Please note any additional comments about the course: _____

_____

Thank you!

Table 6.4   LDE Facilitation Feedback Form

Course: *Noncyclical Standard Work*   Participant Name (Optional): _____

Instructor(s): _____

Date: _____

Thank you for attending this class. Your opinions are important to us. Please take a few minutes to complete this survey. The information collected will be used to ensure the quality of this training program and to continuously improve it.

Course Objectives:

To what extent was each of the following course objectives met for you? Please check the box that best represents your opinion.

	Objective	Rating				
		Fully met	*Mostly met*	*Undecided*	*Somewhat met*	*Not met at all*
1.	Increased understanding of what Noncyclical Standard Work is					
2.	Increased ability to develop a case for using Noncyclical Standard Work					
3.	Increased ability to recognize Noncyclical Standard Work					
4.	Increased skill in identifying barriers to Noncyclical Standard Work and ways to overcome them using Noncyclical Standard Work tools					

Comments: _____
_____

Table 6.4 (continued)   LDE Facilitation Feedback Form

Course Materials:

Please rate the quality of the following items by checking the box that best represents your opinion.

		Rating				
	Item	Very good	Good	Average	Poor	Very poor
1.	Handouts					
2.	Overheads/Slides					
3.	Exercises					

Comments: _____
_____

Course Delivery:

Please rate the effectiveness of the instructor(s) on the following items by checking the box that best represents your opinion.

		Rating				
	Item	Very effective	Effective	Undecided	Ineffective	Very ineffective
1.	Conveying the learning points of the Lean Discipline					
2.	Encouraging participation					
3.	Balancing lecture and discussion					
4.	Giving clear direction for the exercises					
5.	Maintaining a helpful and friendly manner					
6.	Overall rating of this instructor(s)					

Comments: _____
_____

continued

Table 6.4 (continued)   LDE Facilitation Feedback Form

Overall Course Evaluation:

Please rate the following items by checking the box that best represents your opinion.

		Rating				
	Item	*Strongly agree*	*Agree*	*Undecided/ neutral*	*Disagree*	*Strongly disagree*
1.	I have a better understanding of the importance of Noncyclical Standard Work in a Lean System.					
2.	I believe that Noncyclical Standard Work will improve my process/job.					
3.	I am confident that Noncyclical Standard Work can be successfully implemented in my process/job.					

Comments: _____
_____

What, if anything, would prevent you from using Noncyclical Standard Work on your job? _____
_____

Please note any additional comments about the course: _____
_____

Thank you!

Chapter 7

LDE Total Productive Maintenance

Purchasing equipment is a major investment for most companies, so it is only common sense that we have a plan in place to maintain the equipment. You wouldn't buy a home or a car and then do nothing to keep it in shape would you? I certainly hope not.

Total Productive Maintenance (TPM) is defined as the associated and motivated equipment ownership plan used to improve overall equipment effectiveness (OEE), making use of team-based development and implementation of Autonomous, Preventive, and Predictive Maintenance. The ultimate goal of TPM is to eliminate accidents, eliminate equipment losses, increase productivity, improve quality, reduce variation, reduce costs, minimize inventory, create a clean and pleasant working environment, and increase customer satisfaction. In others words, the goal is to maximize the company's investment to get the biggest bang for the buck! We all know that if you do not maintain the equipment, it will invariably break down at the worst possible times—a sort of Murphy's Law, if you will.

I think it is important that we also clarify what Total Productive Maintenance (TPM) is *not*. TPM is not asking operators to carry out dangerous or unsafe acts, demanding additional work to be performed in lieu of other job duties, asking operators to also do Maintenance's job, or relieving the responsibility of the equipment performance from Maintenance and placing it exclusively on operators. Remember this is about teamwork and ownership. Operators need to be involved, as they are usually the first people to know when something is not right with a piece of equipment; after all, they are using or running that piece of equipment every day. I knew an operator who could tell by the sounds his equipment made during a cycle whether or not it was working properly; it may be hard to believe, but it was true!

Total Productive Maintenance LDE Apprentice: The Apprentice section is where candidates receive general overviews not only on their particular Lean discipline, but other Lean activities that work together with their material. If you will notice on the LDE TPM checklist (Table 7.1), the candidate is getting exposure to two other Lean disciplines already. As a TPM LDE Apprentice, it is critical that the candidate capture a true understanding of exactly how TPM ties into all the other Lean disciplines and the overall benefit to the plant. If the candidate has any difficulty in understanding that or the business metrics impacted and how the results are measured, they will need to spend more time in the Apprentice stage. Total Productive Maintenance is not always an easy Lean discipline, and if there is not a solid foundation of Total Productive Maintenance basic understanding before leaving the Apprentice level, the candidate will more than likely have a great deal of difficulty moving forward. The Total Productive Maintenance LDE candidate should begin reading the required materials at this stage as well.

Total Productive Maintenance LDE Generalist: As a TPM LDE Generalist, the candidate will receive comprehensive training in TPM, Excellence in Maintenance, and Autonomous Maintenance, and the candidate will begin to apply these tools and concepts to designated or pilot areas. Carrying over from the LDE Apprentice section, the candidate will also be establishing and implementing baseline Total Productive Maintenance metrics to those areas, being sure to document them for reporting purposes. With the assistance of the Total Productive Maintenance Champion, the candidate will begin teaching, coaching, and mentoring associates in the plant at all levels. Before moving onto the Total Productive Maintenance Specialist level, the candidate will show an understanding of the plant's strategy, mission, and roles as they relate to TPM. The TPM LDE candidate will accomplish this through evidence of implementation, metric performance, and sustainment.

Total Productive Maintenance LDE Specialist: At the Total Productive Maintenance LDE Specialist level, the candidate will be completing many hands-on undertakings, such as conducting process-improvement team workshops* throughout the facility, continuing to implement and sustain Autonomous Maintenance activities throughout the plant, developing TPM standards for equipment and machinery, developing a TPM training plan for the entire facility, leading data collection and TPM analysis, presenting TPM results to the plant staff, and leading all plantwide Total Productive Maintenance events. All the required reading materials should be completed before moving to the TPM Lean Discipline Expert level. The Total Productive Maintenance LDE candidate should always use Table 7.2 whenever facilitating training so they can understand how others perceive them and their communication skills. This is an opportunity for continuous improvement for the candidate.

Total Productive Maintenance LDE Expert: At this stage, the Total Productive Maintenance LDE Expert candidate should have fully developed their facilitation and leadership skills. The candidate should be in a shared leadership role involved with other departments for equipment design, process flows, plant layouts, and design of machinery, especially new equipment and machinery. The TPM LDE Expert candidate should have applied Process Problem Solving tools and practices to eliminate such things as unplanned downtime, reduce or eliminate equipment constraints, balance work in process (WIP) materials between linked processes, and improve Overall Equipment Effectiveness (OEE). The LDE candidate should have documentation showing all of the best practices applied, as well as where those best practices can be applied elsewhere in the facility, and be able to provide documentation where business objectives have been met or exceeded by the application of Total Productive Maintenance programs. The Total Productive Maintenance LDE Expert candidate will develop the long-term plan, vision, and goals for the maintainability of all equipment and machinery and be able to communicate that to all levels of associates in the facility.

---

* A process improvement team workshop simply involves leading a cross-functional group of associates in deconstructing a small or large piece of equipment or machinery, discovering problems and making all necessary repairs, and cleaning and painting the equipment or machinery, ultimately returning it to "like new" condition.

Table 7.1 Total Productive Maintenance Lean Discipline Checklist

Your Company Logo Here	Your Lean System Initials Here	Title: *Training Overview Checklist for TPM LDEs*	Date: August 27, 2014	Rev: 1.0	Page: Page 1 of 1	Document No.: XXX-TPM-7005 Approved by: HR Manager

Starting Date: ____/____/____   Trainee's Name:_____
                                               (Please Print Legibly)

Training Overview Checklist for Total Productive Maintenance LDEs

This training checklist is to be utilized in training Total Productive Maintenance LDEs. Each item needs to be covered by the support personnel listed. As the trainee completes an item, the trainee (T) initials and dates the item. The Lean Manager/Coordinator (LMC) and Plant Manager (PM) initial to indicate that the training is completed.

When a section is completed, the trainee, the Lean Manager/Coordinator, and the Plant Manager initial that the section is complete, verifying that the trainee has attained the designated level of certification.

1. Lean Discipline Apprentice

	T	LMC	PM	Date	
A.	____	____	____	_____	Participate in Total Productive Maintenance Overview class
B.	____	____	____	_____	Participate in Lean Overview training
C.	____	____	____	_____	Complete 5S Overview training
D.	____	____	____	_____	Complete Process Problem Solving Overview training

	T	LMC	PM	Date
Achieved Lean Discipline Apprentice Certification	____	____	____	____

2. Lean Discipline Generalist

	T	LMC	PM	Date	
A.	____	____	____	_____	Complete TPM Train-the-Trainer class
B.	____	____	____	_____	Understand Excellence in Maintenance
C.	____	____	____	_____	Understand mission statement, strategies, and roles

Table 7.1 (continued)   Total Productive Maintenance Lean Discipline Checklist

2. Lean Discipline Generalist (continued)				
	T	**LMC**	**PM**	**Date**
D.	___	___	___	_____	Understand TPM metrics
E.	___	___	___	_____	Initiate problem-solving activities to support TPM

				T	**LMC**	**PM**	**Date**
Achieved Lean Discipline Generalist Certification				_____	_____	_____	_____

3. Lean Discipline Specialist				
	T	**LMC**	**PM**	**Date**
A.	___	___	___	_____	Understand Implementation process for TPM tools and methodologies at the plant level
B.	___	___	___	_____	Achieve LDG certification in: • 5S
C.	___	___	___	_____	• PPS
D.	___	___	___	_____	Lead a Process Improvement Team event
E.	___	___	___	_____	Understand equipment standards
F.	___	___	___	_____	Understand sustaining system for Autonomous Maintenance steps
G.	___	___	___	_____	Understand data collection process to assist with TPM metrics calculations and analysis
H.	___	___	___	_____	Conduct regular PDCA on all areas where TPM has been implemented
I.	___	___	___	_____	Coach on maintenance effectiveness and efficiency
J.	___	___	___	_____	Install or improve Autonomous Maintenance tasks in a specific area

				T	**LMC**	**PM**	**Date**
Achieved Lean Discipline Specialist Certification				_____	_____	_____	_____

continued

Table 7.1 (continued)   Total Productive Maintenance Lean Discipline Checklist

4. Lean Discipline Expert					
	T	**LMC**	**PM**	**Date**	
A.	___	___	___	_____	Assist in the development of TPM strategies/master schedule to support company goals and objectives
B.	___	___	___	_____	Utilize PPS to help eliminate unplanned downtime
C.	___	___	___	_____	Participate in setting TPM goals for management/shop-floor team
D.	___	___	___	_____	Involvement in plant's implementation road map
E.	___	___	___	_____	Participate in changes to facility layout, equipment design, and/or process flow

				CORP	
	T	**LMC**	**PM**	**Apprvl**	**Date**
Achieved Lean Discipline Expert Certification	___	___	___	___	___

Table 7.2   LDE Facilitation Feedback Form

Course: *Total Productive Maintenance*   Participant Name (Optional): _____

Instructor(s): _____

Date: _____

Thank you for attending this class. Your opinions are important to us. Please take a few minutes to complete this survey. The information collected will be used to ensure the quality of this training program and to continuously improve it.

Course Objectives:

To what extent was each of the following course objectives met for you? Please check the box that best represents your opinion.

		Rating				
	Objective	*Fully met*	*Mostly met*	*Undecided*	*Somewhat met*	*Not met at all*
1.	Increased understanding of TPM and how it fits into the Lean system					
2.	Increased ability to explain how TPM works					
3.	Increased ability to identify TPM tools, steps, and concepts					
4.	Increased knowledge of the basic philosophies and principles of TPM					
Comments: _____ _____						

continued

Table 7.2 (continued)   LDE Facilitation Feedback Form

Course Materials:

Please rate the quality of the following items by checking the box that best represents your opinion.

		Rating				
	Item	Very good	Good	Average	Poor	Very poor
1.	Handouts					
2.	Overheads/Slides					
3.	Exercises					

Comments: _____

_____

Course Delivery:

Please rate the effectiveness of the instructor(s) on the following items by checking the box that best represents your opinion.

		Rating				
	Item	Very effective	Effective	Undecided	Ineffective	Very ineffective
1.	Conveying the learning points of the Lean discipline					
2.	Encouraging participation					
3.	Balancing lecture and discussion					
4.	Giving clear direction for the exercises					
5.	Maintaining a helpful and friendly manner					
6.	Overall rating of this instructor(s)					

Comments: _____

_____

Table 7.2 (continued)   LDE Facilitation Feedback Form

Overall Course Evaluation:

Please rate the following items by checking the box that best represents your opinion.

	Item	Rating				
		Strongly agree	Agree	Undecided/ neutral	Disagree	Strongly disagree
1.	I am comfortable with the TPM terminology and tools.					
2.	I am able to determine if and how TPM will improve my manufacturing process.					

Comments: _____
_____

What, if anything, would prevent you from using TPM in your operation? _____

_____

Please note any additional comments about the course: _____

_____

Thank you!

Chapter 8

LDE Quick Changeover/SMED

Quick Changeover (QCO), also known as Single Minute Exchange of Dies (SMED) in some circles, can make a huge impact on quality and cost. Let me share with you a couple of real-life examples I have been involved with.

The first is about a machining operation that ran production seven days a week, 24 hours a day. The machine had 40 stations of operation, and each station had four separate independent spindles. You can imagine the variation potential just for regular production, but add in a complete changeover, and you can probably envision the time constraint involved. The definition of a QCO or SMED process is the time it takes from the making of the last good piece to the first good piece after the changeover. For this particular piece of machining equipment, it was normally between 24 and 32 hours! At the time, we accepted this as normal.

At the same time, the company was being mentored by Toyota, and we soon learned that they had concepts and tools to tackle problems such as this. Working in conjunction with the workers' union, we videotaped the process from a high point in a cherry picker, as this was the only way to see the entire changeover taking place. Upon review of the tapes with a cross-functional team, the opportunity for improvement was very evident. We made a list of actions, created a standardized sequential work checklist of what needed to happen, and then put these activities in place for each changeover. Every time we performed a changeover, we would track the timing on a Pareto chart posted in the work area so that we could all see if the action items were being maintained. After about six months of changeovers with everyone working together and continually making improvements, we got the true changeover time down to 1 hour!

So let's do some math to see the value of this enormous achievement. The machine ran at a rate of 700 pieces an hour, so this was the production lost for each hour of downtime during a changeover. Let's just use the low point of downtime for our example here, which is 24 hours. This equals 16,800 pieces lost each and every changeover, and we were changing over three times a month. This equals a monthly loss of 50,400 pieces! By eliminating the lost production through QCO/SMED techniques, we also eliminated working on Sundays, so now you can also factor in eliminating premium wages for a three-shift crew totaling 27 people and the 18 skilled trades required to cover those three shifts. This amounts to $45 \times 8 = 360$ hours of labor at double-time rates. That is simply amazing to me, and it should be to you too!

The second example is from when I was a senior Supplier Development Engineer assigned to a plastic injection supplier. They were having a lot of difficulty meeting customer demand in a timely manner and were always using premium shipments to deliver to the customer. The supplier was also working seven days a week just to keep up with premium shipments to the customer. Any breakdown in equipment usually meant a shutdown for the customer, as there was absolutely no work in process (WIP) between the supplier and the customer to act as a buffer.

The first item on the agenda was to verify that the equipment capacity could meet customer demand (of course). The cycle time and pieces per cycle were calculated, which showed that the equipment had the capacity to meet the demand and that it should not require seven days a week to do so. After spending some time making observations, there were two opportunities that became apparent. One was Standard Work to reduce product variation and the other was QCO/SMED to stabilize the changeover process. Changeover times were in excess of 24 hours, and it was taking a long time to get the first "good" piece from the equipment where the changeover had taken place. There were 28 pieces of equipment this would have an impact on.

We put a cross-functional team in place and, using the techniques of videotaping and a spaghetti chart, we documented the current changeover process. The team then reviewed all the information and brainstormed ideas and concepts that would be helpful. Using those ideas, a standard work changeover checklist, and the Pareto chart, we moved forward and made a great deal of progress over a relatively short period of time. Within two months, the changeover time, no matter the size of the equipment, was at 45 minutes. The operation was soon stabilized into a five-day-a-week work schedule with an occasional Saturday, and all premium shipments were eliminated. This was big money that the plant could use for other things such as expansion or improvements to current business. One note that I think is worth sharing here is that many of the ideas from the associates had been previously forwarded to management but were ignored. Let's keep those ears open, people!

Quick Changeover/SMED LDE Apprentice: In Table 8.1 you will see that during the LDE Apprentice stage, the candidate receives a basic understanding and overviews of Lean, Quick Changeover, and Standard Work, and the expected outcome is for the LDE Apprentice to realize the benefits to the plant, how to measure QCO/SMED activity, how to develop an implementation strategy, and how to recognize what metrics of the business are impacted. As always, the candidate should be able to understand how QCO/SMED combines with all Lean activity. The candidate should start reading the required materials at the Apprentice stage as well.

Quick Changeover/SMED LDE Generalist: As a QCO/SMED LDE Generalist, the candidate will be exposed to comprehensive training on changeover techniques and apply those learnings in a designated area or areas. The candidate will also understand the company's vision, strategies, and applications for QCO/SMED. With assistance from the QCO/SMED Champion, the candidate will begin training all levels of associates in the plant and be instrumental in developing cross-functional teams throughout the plant. The QCO/SMED LDE Generalist is also responsible for establishing QCO/SMED metrics, collecting data on changeovers, and documenting and communicating areas of opportunities for application. Before moving onto the QCO/SMED LDE Specialist stage, candidates should have proven their proficiency through the substantiation of what they have implemented and sustained.

Quick Changeover/SMED LDE Specialist: At the QCO/SMED Specialist stage, the LDE candidate will complete the required reading materials, achieve LDE Apprentice level in Process Problem Solving and Error Proofing, and achieve LDE Generalist in Standard Work (both categories). The QCO/SMED LDE Generalist will be leading activities throughout the plant and work with the Human Resource Department to assist in developing a plantwide training plan. The candidate will be instrumental in developing QCO/SMED standards for the plant, developing the how-to guideline for improving changeover processes, recording improvements in plant metrics, and developing the ability to articulately communicate these to the plant staff. To ensure sustainment of the gains made, the QCO/SMED LDE candidate will develop the standards to audit effectiveness and standardization of the changeover processes plantwide. The Quick Changeover LDE candidate should always use Table 8.2 whenever facilitating training so they can understand how others perceive them and their communication skills. This is an opportunity for continuous improvement for the candidate.

Quick Changeover/SMED LDE Expert: At the QCO/SMED LDE Expert level, the candidate should be leading all continuous improvement in the plant for QCO/SMED activities and have shared leadership with other departments such as Manufacturing, Maintenance, Engineering, and Purchasing, developing long-term plans for new equipment, incoming new business, and equipment layouts. The candidate will have documentation regarding learned best practices and how they can be applied throughout the facility. Supporting the company vision and goals, the QCO/SMED LDE Expert candidate will develop the strategy and create the schedule for all QCO/SMED activities and be the main resource for these events. The candidate should have been highly influential in meeting or exceeding the goals set by the company as it relates to QCO/SMED applications.

Table 8.1   Quick Changeover/SMED Lean Discipline Checklist

Your Company Logo Here	Your Lean System Initials Here	Title: *Training Overview Checklist for Quick Changeover LDEs*	Date: August 29, 2014	Rev: 1.0	Page: Page 1 of 1	Document No.: XXX-QCO-7006 Approved by: HR Manager

Starting Date: ____/____/____   Trainee's Name:_____
                                              (Please Print Legibly)

Training Overview Checklist for QCO LDEs

This training checklist is to be utilized in training QCO LDEs. Each item needs to be covered by the support personnel listed. As the trainee completes an item, the trainee (T) initials and dates the item. The Lean Manager/Coordinator (LMC) and Plant Manager (PM) initial to indicate that the training is completed.

When a section is completed, the trainee, the Lean Manager/Coordinator, and the Plant Manager initial that the section is complete, verifying that the trainee has attained the designated level of certification.

1. Lean Discipline Apprentice

	T	LMC	PM	Date	
A.	____	____	____	_____	Participate in QCO Overview class
B.	____	____	____	_____	Participate in Lean Overview training
C.	____	____	____	_____	Participate in STD Work overview

	T	LMC	PM	Date
Achieved Lean Discipline Apprentice Certification	_____	_____	_____	_____

2. Lean Discipline Generalist

	T	LMC	PM	Date	
A.	____	____	____	_____	Participate in QCO Train-the-Trainer class
B.	____	____	____	_____	Participate in a QCO event in a pilot area
C.	____	____	____	_____	Collect data in pilot area to help prioritize which opportunities to focus on
D.	____	____	____	_____	Train and develop plant implementation team, plant leadership team, and shop-floor cell teams in a pilot area

continued

Table 8.1 (continued)   Quick Changeover/SMED Lean Discipline Checklist

2. Lean Discipline Generalist (continued)				
	T	**LMC**	**PM**	**Date**	
E.	___	___	___	_____	Understand mission statement, strategies, and roles
F.	___	___	___	_____	Achieve Generalist Certification in Standard Work

	T	**LMC**	**PM**	**Date**
Achieved Lean Discipline Generalist Certification	___	___	___	___

3. Lean Discipline Specialist				
	T	**LMC**	**PM**	**Date**	
A.	___	___	___	_____	Document, analyze, and present results at the facility level to support QCO events
B.	___	___	___	_____	Implement QCO tools in areas plantwide
C.	___	___	___	_____	Use QCO metrics to show improvement through use of QCO tools plantwide
D.	___	___	___	_____	Execute breakout schedule for implementing QCO in an area of the facility
E.	___	___	___	_____	Develop working knowledge of Lean tools and achieve LDA for PPS
F.	___	___	___	_____	Develop working knowledge of Lean tools and achieve LDA for Error Proofing
G.	___	___	___	_____	Set new QCO standards and audit standards on sustainment and effectiveness

	T	**LMC**	**PM**	**Date**
Achieved Lean Discipline Specialist Certification	___	___	___	___

Table 8.1 (continued)   Quick Changeover/SMED Lean Discipline Checklist

4. Lean Discipline Expert					
	T	**LMC**	**PM**	**Date**	
A.	___	___	___	_____	Develop QCO strategies, master schedule, and breakout schedules to support company goals and objectives
B.	___	___	___	_____	Use CI methodology to target and initiate activities for major areas for change where QCO concepts can be applied
C.	___	___	___	_____	Set goals for management/shop-floor team/QCO core team and act as a resource for the core team
D.	___	___	___	_____	Share leadership of facility layouts, machinery equipment design, and process flow for new launches and production moves

		T	LMC	PM	**CORP** Apprvl	Date
Achieved Lean Discipline Expert Certification		___	___	___	___	___

Table 8.2   LDE Facilitation Feedback Form

Course: *Quick Changeover/SMED*   Participant Name (Optional): _____

Instructor(s): _____

Date: _____

Thank you for attending this class. Your opinions are important to us. Please take a few minutes to complete this survey. The information collected will be used to ensure the quality of this training program and to continuously improve it.

Course Objectives:

To what extent was each of the following course objectives met for you? Please check the box that best represents your opinion.

	Objective	Rating				
		Fully met	*Mostly met*	*Undecided*	*Somewhat met*	*Not met at all*
1.	Increased understanding of what Quick Changeover is					
2.	Increased ability to identify Quick Changeover benefits					
3.	Increased ability to recognize Quick Changeover opportunities and implement them					
4.	Increased skill in identifying barriers to Quick Changeover and ways to overcome them					

Comments: _____

_____

Table 8.2 (continued)   LDE Facilitation Feedback Form

Course Materials:

Please rate the quality of the following items by checking the box that best represents your opinion.

		Rating				
	Item	*Very good*	*Good*	*Average*	*Poor*	*Very poor*
1.	Handouts					
2.	Overheads/Slides					
3.	Exercises					

Comments: _____
_____

Course Delivery:

Please rate the effectiveness of the instructor(s) on the following items by checking the box that best represents your opinion.

		Rating				
	Item	*Very effective*	*Effective*	*Undecided*	*Ineffective*	*Very ineffective*
1.	Conveying the learning points of the subject matter					
2.	Encouraging participation					
3.	Balancing lecture and discussion					
4.	Giving clear direction for the exercises					
5.	Maintaining a helpful and friendly manner					
6.	Overall rating of this instructor(s)					

Comments: _____
_____

continued

Table 8.2 (continued)   LDE Facilitation Feedback Form

Overall Course Evaluation:

Please rate the following items by checking the box that best represents your opinion.

		Rating				
	Item	*Strongly agree*	*Agree*	*Undecided/ neutral*	*Disagree*	*Strongly disagree*
1.	I have a better understanding of the importance of Quick Changeover.					
2.	I believe that Quick Changeover will improve my process/job.					
3.	I am confident that Quick Changeover can be successfully implemented in my process/job.					

Comments: _____
_____

What, if anything, would prevent you from using Quick Changeover at your job? __
_____

Please note any additional comments about the course: _____
_____

Thank you!

Chapter 9

Error Detection/Proofing

I personally believe that true Error Proofing can only be achieved through Built In Quality (BIQ), both in the product and process design stages. The Lean Discipline Expert candidate for Error Proofing will in all likelihood start off by dealing with Error Detection to designs, products and processes already in place. The LDE candidate will be very important as they grow, to be placed into the early stages of product and process design to be able to apply what they have learned and achieve true Error Proofing therefore having an impact on Safety, Quality, Cost and other factors such as rework. The investment into any Lean Discipline Expert candidate is minor compared to the amount of positive impact they will make on a company's Key Process Indicators (KPIs).

Many people believe that Error Proofing is defined as an improvement to a process that is designed to prevent defects from occurring. This in reality is the prevention of errors by detection. This may be one or multiple defects that could occur in a process. Error proofing should also foster a technique that is conducive to operator safety, prevents damage to a machine, and of course, prevents defects from being produced or passed on to the next operation or the final customer. Additionally, Error Proofing devices should be simple, low cost, and provide 100% assessment and immediate feedback to an abnormal condition. When I say low cost, I mean you have to weigh the cost of the Error Proofing device against the cost of potential defects made or a recall from the field. A field recall is not only very expensive, but high in cost to customer confidence, and I am not sure you can put a price on that.

The three most common types of inspection are judgment, information, and source inspection. None of these will decrease a company's defect rate.

Error proofing devices should eliminate most forms of human inspection interaction, which is at best only 65% effective at a 300% inspection rate. Yes, that is a fact! We all understand that the greater the human involvement, the greater is the chance for a defect to pass. Error proofing should provide quality at the source by taking a zero-defects approach, relieving operators of monotonous repetition, preventing unintended mistakes, and serving as a device or method that is built into the product or process design to provide an automatic check.

One of the best tools that I know to help you in predicting where Error Proofing may be needed in a design or process is the Failure Mode and Effect Analysis (FMEA). While working in facilities that were having problems with defects, it always amazed me that when I asked to see the FMEA, they either did not know what I was talking about or did not perform one! This happened more than you would think.

There are generally two types of FMEAs—Design and Process—and they should be considered "living" documents that you keep, maintain throughout the life of the process, and review on an annual basis. The FMEA helps you recognize what could go wrong and evaluate what exactly would be the effect. By understanding this, you can ask yourself, "What can we do to prevent the failure or lessen the severity of the consequences?" The purpose of the FMEA is to analyze, develop actions, and create a risk assessment that prioritizes potential problems. There are many types of Error Proofing devices, and here are just a few I have seen or used in many facilities across the globe: guides, interference rods or pins, probe wires, fixture templates, limit switches, microswitches, cameras, electronic sensors, sequence restrictions, gates, stoppers, part-present probes, no part–no cycle, and counters. The earlier in the design of a process or a piece of equipment you can incorporate Error Proofing, the lower its cost it will be. That is another reason I am a firm believer in using the FMEA tool and utilizing a cross-functional group to complete it and review it. A cross-functional group that has experience in a similar process will be the most beneficial, or if it is a new process, then the best cross-functional group would be the engineers, operators, team leaders, etc., who are going to be working that new process.

If your company has FMEAs and/or has any Error Proofing devices incorporated into processes, I would highly recommend that the Error Proofing Lean Discipline Expert candidate(s) should spend time with your engineering group. The Error Proofing LDE should review your FMEAs and go to the Gemba to see the Error Proofing devices in action. I also strongly suggest that the Error Proofing Lean Discipline Expert candidate complete the bulk of the required reading material before completing the LDE Apprentice section. The Error Proofing LDE will receive a great deal of benefit by doing this. When going through the Error Proofing Lean Discipline Expert checklist (Table 9.1) you will see that there is a lot of interaction with the Lean disciplines of Process Problem Solving and Standard Work, as well as learning all about the FMEA process. As you can also see on the Error Proofing Lean Discipline Expert checklist, the candidate starts implementing quickly in the LDE Generalist stage, and at the LDE Expert stage, the candidate becomes the trainer for FMEAs and Error Proofing.

> **Error Proofing LDE Apprentice:** The expected outcome of the Error Proofing LDE candidate at the Apprentice level is for the candidate to have a very good understanding of Error Proofing and how it benefits the total organization, to develop an implementation approach. They should know what business metrics are affected, how Error Proofing integrates with other Lean activities, and how Error Proofing activity is measured.

> **Error Proofing LDE Generalist:** At this point, the Error Proofing Lean Champion will need to provide some hands-on assistance for the Error Proofing Lean Discipline Expert candidate in the areas of developing and training an Error Proofing implementation team, clarifying the facility's Error Proofing strategies and roles, and potentially coaching on the FMEA process, especially Risk Priority Number (RPN), Risk Assessment, Severity, Occurrence, and Detection. The Error Proofing LDE candidate at the Generalist stage will have confirmed competencies in the application of three Error Proofing devices through evidence of implementation, established baseline metrics, understanding the use of Error Proofing devices across the facility, and demonstrating an Error Proofing application to Standard Work.

> **Error Proofing LDE Specialist:** At the Specialist level, the Error Proofing LDE candidate will achieve certification as a Lean Discipline Generalist in Process Problem Solving and Standard Work, complete FMEA training, and present results at the facility level to confirm Error Proofing activities through analyzing data and support documentation. Additionally, at the Specialist level, the Error Proofing Lean Discipline candidate will apply the FMEA process, maintain and record Error Proofing in plant-level metrics, and implement Error Proofing in manufacturing and business process areas. The Error Proofing LDE candidate should always use Table 9.2 whenever facilitating training so they can

understand how others perceive them and their communication skills. This is an opportunity for continuous improvement for the candidate.

Error Proofing LDE Expert: At this level, the Error Proofing LDE candidate can teach, lead, and initiate Error Proofing activities. This candidate should also be able to lead your facility to achieve zero defects; share Error Proofing best practices throughout the organization; develop the Error Proofing strategy and schedule to support company goals and objectives; share the Error Proofing objective with project teams to develop long-term plans for new processes, equipment, or facilities; and meet or exceed Error Proofing business goals. Upon completing this section, the Error Proofing Lean Discipline Expert will be the facilities resource and lead all Error Proofing activities.

Table 9.1   Error Proofing Lean Discipline Expert Checklist

Your Company Logo Here	Your Lean System Initials Here	Title: *Training Overview Checklist for Error Proofing LDEs*	Date: August 31, 2014	Rev: 1.0	Page: Page 1 of 1	Document No.: XXX-EP-7007 **Approved by:** HR Manager

Starting Date: ___/___/___   Trainee's Name:_____
                                                (Please Print Legibly)

Training Overview Checklist for Error Proofing LDEs

This training checklist is to be utilized in training Error Proofing LDEs. Each item needs to be covered by the support personnel listed. As the trainee completes an item, the trainee (T) initials and dates the item. The Lean Manager/Coordinator and Plant Manager (PM) initial to indicate that the training is completed.

When a section is completed, the trainee, the Lean Manager/Coordinator, and the Plant Manager initial that the section is complete, verifying that the trainee has attained the designated level of certification.

1. Lean Discipline Apprentice

	T	LMC	PM	Date	
A.	___	___	___	_____	Participate in Error Proofing Overview Class
B.	___	___	___	_____	Participate in Lean Overview Training
C.	___	___	___	_____	Complete PPS Overview Training
D.	___	___	___	_____	Complete Standard Work Overview Training

Achieved Lean Discipline Apprentice Certification   T ___ LMC ___ PM ___ Date ___

2. Lean Discipline Generalist

	T	LMC	PM	Date	
A.	___	___	___	_____	Complete Error Proofing Training (8 hr)
B.	___	___	___	_____	Understand Error Proofing mission statement, strategy, and roles
C.	___	___	___	_____	Implement three Error Proofing solutions
D.	___	___	___	_____	Basic understanding of FMEAs

Achieved Lean Discipline Generalist Certification   T ___ LMC ___ PM ___ Date ___

continued

Table 9.1 (continued)   Error Proofing Lean Discipline Expert Checklist

3. **Lean Discipline Specialist**				
	T	**LMC**	**PM**	**Date**	
A.	___	___	___	_____	Complete Error Proofing Train-the-Trainer class
B.	___	___	___	_____	Complete FMEA Training
C.	___	___	___	_____	Understand Error Proofing implementation process
D.	___	___	___	_____	Obtain LDG level for PPS
E.	___	___	___	_____	Obtain LDG level for Standard Work
F.	___	___	___	_____	Understand and Explain Plant-Related Metrics
G.	___	___	___	_____	Understand Error Proofing standard

	T	**LMC**	**PM**	**Date**
Achieved Lean Discipline Specialist Certification	_____	_____	_____	_____

4. **Lean Discipline Expert**				
	T	**LMC**	**PM**	**Date**	
A.	___	___	___	_____	Participate in developing Error Proofing strategies to support goals
B.	___	___	___	_____	Trainer for FMEA
C.	___	___	___	_____	Lead Error Proofing Training

	T	**LMC**	**PM**	**CORP Apprvl**	**Date**
Achieved Lean Discipline Expert Certification	_____	_____	_____	_____	_____

Table 9.2 LDE Facilitation Feedback Form

Course: *Error Proofing*   Participant Name (Optional): _____

Instructor(s): _____

Date: _____

Thank you for attending this class. Your opinions are important to us. Please take a few minutes to complete this survey. The information collected will be used to ensure the quality of this training program and to continuously improve it.

Course Objectives:

To what extent was each of the following course objectives met for you? Please check the box that best represents your opinion.

	Objective	Rating				
		Fully met	*Mostly met*	*Undecided*	*Somewhat met*	*Not met at all*
1.	Increased understanding of what Error Proofing is					
2.	Increased ability to identify Error Proofing benefits					
3.	Increased ability to recognize Error Proofing opportunities and implement them					
4.	Increased skill in identifying barriers to Error Proofing and ways to overcome them					
Comments: _____ _____						

continued

Table 9.2 (continued)   LDE Facilitation Feedback Form

Course Materials:

Please rate the quality of the following items by checking the box that best represents your opinion.

	Item	Rating				
		Very good	Good	Average	Poor	Very poor
1.	Handouts					
2.	Overheads/Slides					
3.	Exercises					

Comments: _____
_____

Course Delivery:

Please rate the effectiveness of the instructor(s) on the following items by checking the box that best represents your opinion.

	Item	Rating				
		Very effective	Effective	Undecided	Ineffective	Very ineffective
1.	Conveying the learning points of the subject matter					
2.	Encouraging participation					
3.	Balancing lecture and discussion					
4.	Giving clear direction for the exercises					
5.	Maintaining a helpful and friendly manner					
6.	Overall rating of this instructor(s)					

Comments: _____
_____

Table 9.2 (continued)   LDE Facilitation Feedback Form

Overall Course Evaluation:

Please rate the following items by checking the box that best represents your opinion.

		Rating				
	Item	*Strongly agree*	*Agree*	*Undecided/ neutral*	*Disagree*	*Strongly disagree*
1.	I have a better understanding of the importance of Error Proofing.					
2.	I believe that Error Proofing will improve my process/job.					
3.	I am confident that Error Proofing can be successfully implemented in my process/job.					

Comments: _____
_____

What, if anything, would prevent you from using Error Proofing at your job?_____
_____

Please note any additional comments about the course: _____
_____

Thank you!

Chapter 10

LDE Process Problem Solving

From the perspective of this Lean discipline, a solid definition of a *problem* would be an abnormality that varies from the desired or expected condition that should be viewed as an *opportunity* and as a normal part of business (e.g., management, HR, manufacturing). In my opinion, the key words in that definition are *abnormality* and *expected condition*. Do not blame the problem on the people; problems occur because of a system or process failure! The root problem is that either (a) the established standards/procedures were not being followed, (b) the established standards/procedures were wrong, or (c) there was no defined standard.

Process Problem Solving is therefore defined as a structured method to determine the quickest, most cost effective way to ensure that the root cause of a problem is identified, addressed, and permanently eliminated. Problems will generally fall into five categories: safety, quality, quantity, cost, and human relations. Problems generally can also be grouped into four groups: start-up, gradual, sudden, and reoccurring.

I think we can all agree that problems do happen in the real world of things and may be caused by compound interactions and numerous variables. Although many times problems seem to be mysterious, that does not mean they are unsolvable. They have definite and physical clues and should be described in terms of facts, standard tools, and documented measurements. There are many Process Problem Solving tools that your Process Problem Solving Lean Discipline Expert candidate will need to be exposed to in order to be effective as an LDE. These are just a few: Statistical Process Controls (SPC), A3s, Pareto charts, Six Sigma (Define, Measure, Analyze, Improve,

Control), Design of Experiments, flow diagrams, check sheets, 5 Why, and 8 Disciplines (8D).

If your company does not already have one, I would like to recommend a good standard for Process Problem Solving steps that your Process Problem Solving Expert candidate may find useful. These steps are

1. Problem selection
2. Containment (if necessary)
3. Problem description
4. Cause analysis
5. Root cause
6. Corrective action
7. Evaluation of corrective action
8. Problem prevention

Process Problem Solving (PPS) Lean Discipline Expert Apprentice:
The PPS LDE Apprentice will need to start with some basic Lean training, as shown in the first section of the PPS LDE checklist (Table 10.1), along with another Lean discipline that usually interacts with PPS, i.e., Standard Work. The PPS LDE candidate needs to start on the required reading materials as soon as possible to begin their education on the various Problem Solving Tools and their application. Upon certification at the Apprentice level, the PPS LDE candidate will have a solid understanding of Process Problem Solving and how it benefits the entire organization, develop an implementation approach, know what business metrics are affected, and know how to measure Process Problem Solving activity.

Process Problem Solving (PPS) Lean Discipline Expert Generalist:
At the Generalist level, the PPS LDE candidate will begin applying and implementing PPS tools with the assistance of the Process Problem Solving Lean Champion. I am a firm believer that nothing beats hands-on training, so this level of activity is really great exposure for the PPS LDE candidate. As a certified Process Problem Solving Lean Discipline Generalist, the candidate will have launched baseline Process Problem Solving metrics for the facility, established data collection procedures in the work areas to identify opportunities for application of Process Problem Solving, and demonstrated to the plant staff confirmation of their competencies in applying Process Problem Solving tools through evidence of implementation and results.

Process Problem Solving (PPS) Lean Discipline Specialist: At the Specialist level, the PPS LDE candidates will begin to establish themselves as the go-to resource for the facility in regard to Process Problem Solving issues. The candidate's expertise in PPS documentation and tools selection continues to grow in various areas throughout the facility. This growth will be documented in the plant metrics. Upon certification as a PPS LDE Specialist, the candidate will have a clear understanding of the relationship among Lean tools and how Lean tools support the business objectives, and the candidate will also be the leader for Process Problem Solving activities throughout the facility. The Process Problem Solving LDE candidate should always use Table 10.2 whenever facilitating training so they can understand how others perceive them and their communication skills. This is an opportunity for continuous improvement for the candidate.

Process Problem Solving (PPS) Lean Discipline Expert: As a certified Process Problem Solving Lean Discipline Expert, the candidate will teach, lead, coach, and initiate the facility's Process Problem Solving activities. The PPS LDEs will have developed themselves as experts in the understanding of problem definition, root cause analysis, and short- and long-term countermeasures, and they will know how to apply advanced problem-solving techniques, including Six Sigma and Design of Experiments. The PPS LDE will also take a position of shared leadership with regard to facility layouts, machinery and equipment design, and process flows.

Table 10.1   Process Problem Solving Lean Discipline Checklist

Your Company Logo Here	Your Lean System Initials Here	Title: *Training Overview Checklist for Process Problem Solving LDEs*	Date: *September 27, 2014*	Rev: 1.0	Page: Page 1 of 1	Document No.: XXX-PPS-7008 Approved by: HR Manager

Starting Date: ____/____/____   Trainee's Name:_____

(Please Print Legibly)

Training Overview Checklist for Process Problem Solving LDEs

This training checklist is to be utilized in training Process Problem Solving LDEs. Each item needs to be covered by the support personnel listed. As the trainee completes an item, the trainee (T) initials and dates the item. The Lean Manager/Coordinator (LMC) and Plant Manager (PM) initial to indicate that the training is completed.

When a section is completed, the trainee, the Lean Manager/Coordinator, and the Plant Manager initial that the section is complete, verifying that the trainee has attained the designated level of certification.

1. Lean Discipline Apprentice

	T	LMC	PM	Date	
A.	____	____	____	_____	Participate in Process Problem Solving Overview Class
B.	____	____	____	_____	Lean Overview Training
C.	____	____	____	_____	Complete Standard Work Overview Training

	T	LMC	PM	Date
Achieved Lean Discipline Apprentice Certification	_____	_____	_____	_____

Table 10.1 (continued)   Process Problem Solving Lean Discipline Checklist

2. Lean Discipline Generalist

	T	LMC	PM	Date	
A.	___	___	___	_____	Complete PPS Training (8 hr)
B.	___	___	___	_____	Apply PPS tools in the following areas: • Maintenance
C.	___	___	___	_____	• Quality
D.	___	___	___	_____	• Safety
E.	___	___	___	_____	• Production
F.	___	___	___	_____	Understand Lean Policy Deployment
G.	___	___	___	_____	Understand PPS mission statement, strategy, and roles

	T	LMC	PM	Date
Achieved Lean Discipline Generalist Certification	___	___	___	___

3. Lean Discipline Specialist

	T	LMC	PM	Date	
A.	___	___	___	_____	Document, analyze, and present results of PPS activities
B.	___	___	___	_____	Complete overview training for Six Sigma and DOE
C.	___	___	___	_____	Understand PPS implementation process
D.	___	___	___	_____	Complete PPS Train-the-Trainer class
E.	___	___	___	_____	Obtain LDG level for 5S
F.	___	___	___	_____	Obtain LDG level for Standard Work
G.	___	___	___	_____	Utilize PPS problem solving tools (2 minimum)

	T	LMC	PM	Date
Achieved Lean Discipline Specialist Certification	___	___	___	___

continued

Table 10.1 (continued)   Process Problem Solving Lean Discipline Checklist

4.	**Lean Discipline Expert**				
	T	**LMC**	**PM**	**Date**	
A.	___	___	___	_____	Assist in the development of PPS strategies to support company goals and objectives
B.	___	___	___	_____	Act as a resource for PPS teams
C.	___	___	___	_____	Utilize PPS to effectively address a chronic issue
					Develop an expert understanding of the following:
D.	___	___	___	_____	• Problem definition
E.	___	___	___	_____	• Root-cause analysis
F.	___	___	___	_____	• Short- and long-term countermeasures
					Understand advanced problem solving tools:
G.	___	___	___	_____	• Six Sigma
H.	___	___	___	_____	• Design of Experiments

				CORP	
	T	**LMC**	**PM**	**Apprvl**	**Date**
Achieved Lean Discipline Expert Certification	___	___	___	___	___

Table 10.2 LDE Facilitation Feedback Form

Course: *Process Problem Solving*   Participant Name (Optional): _____

Instructor(s): _____

Date: _____

Thank you for attending this class. Your opinions are important to us. Please take a few minutes to complete this survey. The information collected will be used to ensure the quality of this training program and to continuously improve it.

Course Objectives:

To what extent was each of the following course objectives met for you? Please check the box that best represents your opinion.

	Objective	Rating				
		Fully met	*Mostly met*	*Undecided*	*Somewhat met*	*Not met at all*
1.	Increased understanding of what Process Problem Solving is					
2.	Increased ability to identify Process Problem Solving benefits					
3.	Increased ability to recognize Process Problem Solving opportunities and implement them					
4.	Increased skill in identifying barriers to Process Problem Solving and ways to overcome them					
Comments: _____ _____						

continued

Table 10.2 (continued)   LDE Facilitation Feedback Form

Course Materials:

Please rate the quality of the following items by checking the box that best represents your opinion.

	Item	Rating				
		Very good	Good	Average	Poor	Very poor
1.	Handouts					
2.	Overheads/Slides					
3.	Exercises					

Comments: _____
_____

Course Delivery:

Please rate the effectiveness of the instructor(s) on the following items by checking the box that best represents your opinion.

	Item	Rating				
		Very effective	Effective	Undecided	Ineffective	Very ineffective
1.	Conveying the learning points of the subject matter					
2.	Encouraging participation					
3.	Balancing lecture and discussion					
4.	Giving clear direction for the exercises					
5.	Maintaining a helpful and friendly manner					
6.	Overall rating of this instructor(s)					

Comments: _____
_____

Table 10.2 (continued)   LDE Facilitation Feedback Form

Overall Course Evaluation:

Please rate the following items by checking the box that best represents your opinion.

	Item	Rating				
		Strongly agree	*Agree*	*Undecided/ neutral*	*Disagree*	*Strongly disagree*
1.	I have a better understanding of the importance of Process Problem Solving.					
2.	I believe that Process Problem Solving will improve my process/job.					
3.	I am confident that Process Problem Solving can be successfully implemented in my process/job.					

Comments: _____
_____

What, if anything, would prevent you from using Process Problem Solving at your job?_____
_____

Please note any additional comments about the course: _____
_____

Thank you!

Chapter 11

LDE Material Management

I have a question for you: If our material costs are approximately 68%–75% of our total cost and our labor cost is approximately 7%, why do some businesses focus on layoffs or reducing headcount instead of managing their materials from the supplier to the customer, where the larger cost is? Could it be because implementing a world-class material management system is impossible or too difficult? Well, I think Toyota and others have proven to the world that it is neither! They have become experts at implementing and sustaining material management tools such as Kanban, Changeover Wheel, Pull, JIT, and Plan For Every Part (PFEP), to name just a few. A Material Management Lean Discipline Expert could easily save you hundreds of thousands of dollars.

The purpose of Material Management is to implement a process that effectively moves material through the manufacturing operations to support the material flow strategy, resulting in the delivery of the right part, in the right quantity, at the right time required by the customer. Keep in mind the definition of the *customer*: The customer can be located in many locations of any process in addition to the final customer. This requires an across-the-board set of guidelines and standards all the way from the supplier to the final delivery point. I believe that we can all agree that excess material not only ties up a lot of working capital, but in a global competitive market, it could ultimately cost customer business. Beyond this, excess material also hides problems in the facility, such as poor quality and poor scheduling.

Early in my career, I was a buyer for certain manufacturing components used in an assembly process. The very first thing I was told and taught was *never* to shut down production due to a lack of material. Can you imagine how many days of material on hand that relates to? Usually it meant 30 days or sometimes more if the supplier was overseas. I was one of four buyers for manufacturing, so you can imagine how much capital was tied up because of that mentality!

I was also a production supervisor for a number of years and worked in many different types of processes, one of which was a machining operation that produced eight different part numbers. These parts went from my department to other departments for more machining and subassembly work. We did receive a schedule from Production Control and Logistics, but what I was told and taught was, again, *never* stop running these machines! It didn't matter if the parts were needed downstream; you just kept producing, and usually the general foreman would tell me which parts to run. This was because we were on an efficiency pay-point production system; in other words, I had to produce a certain quantity of parts to justify my headcount, and each part number had a different pay point. The general foreman really liked hitting an efficiency of 105% to 109% every day, so I ran the parts that would achieve that number on a daily basis.

The two examples of material and cash waste are generally accepted as the old way of doing business, but there are still companies out there that use this mantra, and truthfully, I don't know how they survive in business, and I know of several that didn't. I hope those two case examples have you cringing and thinking that this is not the right way to do business or survive your competition. I also hope that this may help you see why the Material Management Lean Discipline Expert can be a key to your success in applying Lean. So be smart and implement a Material Management process that supports the material flow strategy by moving material from the supplier, through the plant, and to all the customers in the smallest lot possible to meet customer demand. Don't forget what your competition is hoping for—that you will do nothing. Be tireless and push the need for continuous improvement. Never be satisfied with whatever Material Management process you have now.

Material Management (MM) LDE Apprentice: Initially the Material Management Lean Discipline Expert candidate will be exposed to a great deal of training in Material Management and several other Lean discipline categories such as 5S, Standard Work, and Process Problem Solving. Remember, the Lean disciplines overlap; we are not trying to cherry pick disciplines. This exposure will be very beneficial, as the LDE candidate learns of tools to apply to a Material Management process. Upon completion of the Material Management Lean Discipline Apprentice level, the candidate will have an understanding of Material Management, the metrics affected, and how it benefits the organization. The candidate will also have developed an implementation approach and learned how to measure Material Management activities.

Material Management (MM) LDE Generalist: At the Generalist level, the Material Management LDE checklist (Table 11.1) mentions two types of specialized training. One is CCF (Red Book), which stands for Creating Continuous Flow, and the other is MMF (Green Book), which stands for Making Materials Flow. These courses are only offered through Mr. Rick Harris, president of Harris Lean Systems (http:// harrisleansystems.com) and are two of the best Material Management training sessions I have come across. You can schedule a training session at your facility (I believe that they require a minimum number of participants), or you can send your Material Management Lean Discipline Expert candidate to their location to participate with others. The books are also listed in the Lean Library in Chapter 13, but the training sessions are a major key to the understanding of your MM LDE.

Also at the Generalist level, the candidate gets exposed to a Material Management tool called the Plan For Every Part (PFEP). A Plan For Every Part is a material planning process that identifies and creates a detailed material flow plan for every part in the supply chain. The data required to create, maintain, and improve the plan is stored in a spreadsheet application such as Excel. The plan begins with the customer and works back through to the supplier with the goal of supporting the operators and eliminating waste in the supply chain. The PFEP becomes the DNA of your facility through the database that is created to gather and maintain information about *all* part numbers in the manufacturing process with information such as (but not limited to) part numbers, usage volume, all of the locations in the facility where the part might reside, packaging type, packaging dimensions, quantity contained within each package, and detailed supplier information. In my opinion, the PFEP is a required tool for the success of any Material Management system.

Upon completion of the Generalist level, the Material Management Lean Discipline Expert candidate will understand the facility's vision, strategies, and roles regarding Material Management and will have successfully applied a variety of Material Management tools in predetermined work areas. With internal assistance, the MM LDE will have trained leadership members and cross-functional associates for the work environment and will have established documented metrics for the facility regarding its Material Management system.

Material Management (MM) LDE Specialist: At the Specialist level, the Material Management LDE candidate will now implement without assistance and track the documented metrics. The Specialist will report on the progress of implementation as well as sustainment on a regular basis to the plant staff. The candidate will also expand the implementation of Material Management tools into the nonmanufacturing areas such as MRO and office-type materials. Upon completion of the Specialist level, the Material Management Lean Discipline Expert candidate will be certified as a Generalist in 5S and Standard Work and will develop Material Management standards throughout the facility to maintain effectiveness. The Material Management LDE candidate should always use Table 11.2 whenever facilitating training so they can understand how others perceive them and their communication skills. This is an opportunity for continuous improvement for the candidate.

Material Management (MM) LDE Expert: At the expert level, the MM LDE will have developed the necessary facilitation skills to communicate, teach, guide, coach, and lead Material Management activity across the facility. Additionally, the MM LDE at this level will develop a Material Management strategy and a schedule that supports company goals and objectives, and will be a resource to the leadership team while sharing leadership of facility layouts, machinery and equipment design, and process flows. The Material Management Lean Discipline Expert will maintain documentation on the best practices and communicate these across the company, meet or exceed the business objectives and goals presented to them, and be able to share the organization's Material Management vision with project teams to develop long-term plans for new processes, equipment, or facilities.

Table 11.1   Material Management Lean Discipline Checklist

Your Company Logo Here	Your Lean System Initials Here	Title: *Training Overview Checklist for Material Management LDEs*	Date: *September 29, 2014*	Rev: 1.0	Page: Page 1 of 1	Document No.: XXX-IM-7011 Approved by: HR Manager

Starting Date: ____/____/____   Trainee's Name:_____
(Please Print Legibly)

Training Overview Checklist for Material Management LDEs

This training checklist is to be utilized in training Material Management LDEs. Each item needs to be covered by the support personnel listed. As the trainee completes an item, the trainee (T) initials and dates the item. The Lean Manager/Coordinator (LMC) and Plant Manager (PM) initial to indicate that the training is completed.

When a section is completed, the trainee, the Lean Manager/Coordinator, and the Plant Manager initial that the section is complete, verifying that the trainee has attained the designated level of certification.

1. Lean Discipline Apprentice

	T	LMC	PM	Date	
A.	____	____	____	_____	Complete Material Management Overview Class
B.	____	____	____	_____	Complete Lean Overview Training
C.	____	____	____	_____	Complete 5S Overview Training
D.	____	____	____	_____	Complete Standard Work Overview Training
E.	____	____	____	_____	Complete PPS Overview Training

	T	LMC	PM	Date
Achieved Lean Discipline Apprentice Certification	_____	_____	_____	_____

continued

Table 11.1 (continued)   Material Management Lean Discipline Checklist

2. Lean Discipline Generalist

	T	LMC	PM	Date	
A.	___	___	___	_____	Participate in CCF and MMF classes for Material Management
B.	___	___	___	_____	Understand mission statement, strategies, and roles
C.	___	___	___	_____	Implement MM tools in a designated pilot area, including a PFEP
D.	___	___	___	_____	Understand MM metrics
E.	___	___	___	_____	Achieve Generalist in 5S
F.	___	___	___	_____	Achieve Generalist in Standard Work

		T	LMC	PM	Date
Achieved Lean Discipline Generalist Certification		_____	_____	_____	_____

3. Lean Discipline Specialist

	T	LMC	PM	Date	
A.	___	___	___	_____	Document, analyze, and present results of MM activities
B.	___	___	___	_____	Implement MM tools in all factories/cells in the plant
C.	___	___	___	_____	Understand MM implementation
D.	___	___	___	_____	Understand MM standards and sustaining systems

		T	LMC	PM	Date
Achieved Lean Discipline Specialist Certification		_____	_____	_____	_____

Table 11.1 (continued)   Material Management Lean Discipline Checklist

4. **Lean Discipline Expert**				
	T	LMC	PM	Date	
A.	___	___	___	_____	Participate in the development of the plant master schedule
B.	___	___	___	_____	Develop breakout schedules to support MM objectives
C.	___	___	___	_____	Identify Kaizen activities in MM areas
D.	___	___	___	_____	Be recognized as a resource to plant teams
E.	___	___	___	_____	Participate in facility layouts, machine design, and process flow improvements

				CORP	
	T	LMC	PM	Apprvl	Date
Achieved Lean Discipline Expert Certification	___	___	___	___	___

Table 11.2   LDE Facilitation Feedback Form

Course: *Material Management*   Participant Name (Optional): _____

Instructor(s): _____

Date: _____

Thank you for attending this class. Your opinions are important to us. Please take a few minutes to complete this survey. The information collected will be used to ensure the quality of this training program and to continuously improve it.

Course Objectives:

To what extent was each of the following course objectives met for you? Please check the box that best represents your opinion.

	Objective	Rating				
		Fully met	*Mostly met*	*Undecided*	*Somewhat met*	*Not met at all*
1.	Increased understanding of how MM supports my organization					
2.	Increased ability to explain how an MM system works					
3.	Increased ability to identify the different types of MM and the purpose for each					
4.	Increased knowledge of the factors to consider when creating a MM system					

Comments: _____

_____

Table 11.2 (continued)   LDE Facilitation Feedback Form

Course Materials:

Please rate the quality of the following items by checking the box that best represents your opinion.

	Item	Rating				
		Very good	*Good*	*Average*	*Poor*	*Very poor*
1.	Handouts					
2.	Overheads/Slides					
3.	Exercises					

Comments: _____
_____

Course Delivery:

Please rate the effectiveness of the instructor(s) on the following items by checking the box that best represents your opinion.

	Item	Rating				
		Very effective	*Effective*	*Undecided*	*Ineffective*	*Very ineffective*
1.	Conveying the learning points of the subject matter					
2.	Encouraging participation					
3.	Balancing lecture and discussion					
4.	Giving clear direction for the exercises					
5.	Maintaining a helpful and friendly manner					
6.	Overall rating of this instructor(s)					

Comments: _____
_____

continued

Table 11.2 (continued)   LDE Facilitation Feedback Form

Overall Course Evaluation:

Please rate the following items by checking the box that best represents your opinion.

		Rating				
	Item	*Strongly agree*	*Agree*	*Undecided/ neutral*	*Disagree*	*Strongly disagree*
1.	I am comfortable with the MM terminology.					
2.	I am able to determine if and how a MM system will help me improve my process.					

Comments: _____
_____

What, if anything, would prevent you from using MM in your operation?_____

_____

Please note any additional comments about the course: _____

_____

Thank you!

Chapter 12

LDE Continuous Improvement

I was a member of the Divisional Lean Team at one company, and we were being mentored heavily by Toyota. During a visit to Toyota, they took me to one particular area that had held seven Kaizen events. With things changing so fast, I wondered how the workers would keep pace. My host explained that the Kaizen events were not held one right after another, but only after the expected results were verified to be achieved, standardized, and stabilized. Only then could another Kaizen event be scheduled.

That lesson was applied many times while I worked for that particular company. I knew of a materials supermarket that had nine Kaizen events before the highest results were achieved, and there was a manufacturing cell at one of our Mexican facilities that had eight Kaizen events before they were satisfied that they had gotten the best results possible for that cell. When you think of the philosophy behind this, it is fairly simple. Don't try to eat the proverbial elephant all at one time; eat in smaller pieces, and soon it will be gone.

Continuous Improvement LDE Apprentice: As you review the Lean Discipline Expert Continuous Improvement checklist (Table 12.1) by section, you will notice more discipline exposure than some of the other LDE checklists. This is because of the broader knowledge and experience a Continuous Improvement LDE candidate will need to be effective. A good portion of the basic understanding outcome at the Apprentice level is (a) to think of developing an implementation approach as well as measuring and metrics for Continuous Improvement, (b) to realize how Continuous Improvement benefits the organization, and (c) to realize how Continuous Improvement fits into the overall Lean implementation based upon all the subject overviews contained at the LDE Apprentice level. The candidate should start reading the required material for Continuous Improvement LDEs.

Continuous Improvement LDE Generalist: After completing the Generalist level, the LDE should have a comprehensive understanding of the Continuous Improvement discipline due to extensive training, and should understand the roles, company strategy, and mission and/or vision statements as they relate to Continuous Improvement planning. The candidate at this level is expected to apply tools and models in select areas, as well as developing and implementing Continuous Improvement metrics for those areas. The candidate is also expected to use the PDCA tool to confirm desired results, metric achievement, and sustainment where Continuous Improvement has been applied. The candidate at this level should be able to train associates and groups at all levels as well as develop a written plan for Continuous Improvement in a work area and for a piece of equipment.

Continuous Improvement LDE Specialist: At the completion of the Specialist level, the Continuous Improvement LDE candidate will also have achieved the level of LDE Generalist for Standard Work, Total Productive Maintenance, Process Problem Solving, Error Proofing, Quick Changeover, and Inventory Management—no small task! Think of how much support this candidate can provide for other LDE candidates in those particular disciplines and within the plant itself. The Continuous Improvement candidate will, like all other LDEs (no matter what the discipline), learn how to document, based upon data collection methods developed by the candidate, regular PDCA walks through areas where Continuous Improvement events have occurred and report results to the plant leadership. The candidate should be able to develop methodologies that will highlight the areas where Continuous Improvement activity is needed and prioritize the areas with the greatest need. The Continuous Improvement LDE candidate should have completed all required reading materials before completing the Specialist level. The Continuous Improvement LDE candidate should always use Table 12.2 whenever facilitating training so they can understand how others perceive them and their communication skills. This is an opportunity for continuous improvement for the candidate.

Continuous Improvement LDE Expert: At the LDE Expert level, the candidates should be developing their facilitation skills in communications, leading activities, teaching, guiding, and coaching other associates at any level in the organization. The candidate should also be able to develop and schedule company goals, objects, targets, and strategies for Continuous Improvement activities, as well as identify major opportunities, schedule events for those opportunities, share the vision with plant leadership, and lead the exercises to completion. These areas should include machinery, design of equipment, plant layouts, and process flows for people, materials, and information, to name just a few.

Table 12.1   Continuous Improvement Lean Discipline Expert Checklist

Your Company Logo Here	Your Lean System Initials Here	Title: *Training Overview Checklist for CI LDEs*	Date: *August 14, 2014*	Rev: 1.0	Page: Page 1 of 1	Document No.: XXX-CI-7012 Approved by: HR Manager

Starting Date: ___/___/___   Trainee's Name:_____

                                                        (Please Print Legibly)

Training Overview Checklist for CI LDEs

This training checklist is to be utilized in training Continuous Improvement LDEs. Each item needs to be covered by the support personnel listed. As the trainee completes an item, the trainee (T) initials and dates the item. The Lean Manager/Coordinator (LMC) and Plant Manager (PM) initial to indicate that the training is completed.

When a section is completed, the trainee, the Lean Manager/Coordinator, and the Plant Manager initial that the section is complete, verifying that the trainee has attained the designated level of certification.

1. Lean Discipline Apprentice

	T	LMC	PM	Date	
A.	___	___	___	_____	Participate in a CI Overview Class
B.	___	___	___	_____	Participate in Lean Boot Camp/Lean Overview Training
C.	___	___	___	_____	Participate in 5S, STD Work, PPS, Error Proofing, QCO, and IM overview training

	T	LMC	PM	Date
Achieved Lean Discipline Apprentice Certification	___	___	___	___

2. Lean Discipline Generalist

	T	LMC	PM	Date	
A.	___	___	___	_____	Participate in a CI Train-the-Trainer class
B.	___	___	___	_____	Train and develop plant implementation team, plant leadership team, and shop-floor cell teams in a pilot area

Table 12.1 (continued)   Continuous Improvement Lean Discipline Expert Checklist

2. Lean Discipline Generalist (continued)

	T	LMC	PM	Date	
C.	____	____	____	_____	Use 10-step CI methodologies to independently implement a major (five-day event) change in pilot area
D.	____	____	____	_____	Understand mission statement, strategies, and roles
E.	____	____	____	_____	Use data collection methods to highlight CI opportunities in a pilot area
F.	____	____	____	_____	Develop a plan for Work and Equipment CI events in designated pilot area
G.	____	____	____	_____	Achieve Lean Discipline Generalist in Standard Work
H.	____	____	____	_____	Achieve Lean Discipline Generalist in Process Problem Solving

	T	LMC	PM	Date
Achieved Lean Discipline Generalist Certification	____	____	____	____

3. Lean Discipline Specialist

	T	LMC	PM	Date	
A.	____	____	____	_____	Document, analyze, and present results at the facility level to support CI events
B.	____	____	____	_____	Execute Breakout Schedule for CI events plantwide
C.	____	____	____	_____	Achieve Lean Discipline Generalist in TPM
D.	____	____	____	_____	Achieve Lean Discipline Generalist in QCO
E.	____	____	____	_____	Achieve Lean Discipline Generalist in Error Proofing
F.	____	____	____	_____	Use data collection methods to highlight CI opportunities plantwide

continued

Table 12.1 (continued)   Continuous Improvement Lean Discipline Expert Checklist

3. Lean Discipline Specialist (continued)				
	T	**LMC**	**PM**	**Date**	
G.	___	___	___	_____	Develop a plan for Work and Equipment CI events plantwide
H.	___	___	___	_____	Perform regular audits on changes to confirm results

	T	**LMC**	**PM**	**Date**
Achieved Lean Discipline Specialist Certification	_____	_____	_____	_____

4. Lean Discipline Expert				
	T	**LMC**	**PM**	**Date**	
A.	___	___	___	_____	Develop CI strategies, master schedule, and breakout schedules to support company goals and objectives
B.	___	___	___	_____	Use CI methodology to target and initiate activities for major areas for change
C.	___	___	___	_____	Develop log of all CI events for future use by company personnel across sites
D.	___	___	___	_____	Achieve Lean Discipline Generalist in IM
E.	___	___	___	_____	Set goals for management/shop-floor team/CI Core Team and act as a resource for the core team
F.	___	___	___	_____	Share leadership of facility layouts, machinery equipment design, and process flow for new launches and production moves

	T	**LMC**	**PM**	**CORP Apprvl**	**Date**
Achieved Lean Discipline Expert Certification	_____	_____	_____	_____	_____

Table 12.2   LDE Facilitation Feedback Form

Course: *Continuous Improvement*   Participant Name (Optional): _____

Instructor(s): _____

Date: _____

Thank you for attending this class. Your opinions are important to us. Please take a few minutes to complete this survey. The information collected will be used to ensure the quality of this training program and to continuously improve it.

Course Objectives:

To what extent was each of the following course objectives met for you? Please check the box that best represents your opinion.

	Objective	Rating				
		Fully met	*Mostly met*	*Undecided*	*Somewhat met*	*Not met at all*
1.	Increased understanding of what Continuous Improvement is					
2.	Increased ability to identify the process and benefits of Continuous Improvement					
3.	Increased ability to identify necessary Continuous Improvement preconditions					
4.	Increased ability to explain the purpose and necessity of Continuous Improvement					

Comments: _____

_____

continued

Table 12.2 (continued)   LDE Facilitation Feedback Form

Course Materials:

Please rate the quality of the following items by checking the box that best represents your opinion.

		Rating				
	Item	*Very good*	*Good*	*Average*	*Poor*	*Very poor*
1.	Handouts					
2.	Overheads/Slides					
3.	Exercises					

Comments: _____
_____

Course Delivery:

Please rate the effectiveness of the instructor(s) on the following items by checking the box that best represents your opinion.

		Rating				
	Item	*Very effective*	*Effective*	*Undecided*	*Ineffective*	*Very ineffective*
1.	Conveying the learning points of the Lean discipline					
2.	Encouraging participation					
3.	Balancing lecture and discussion					
4.	Giving clear direction for the exercises					
5.	Maintaining a helpful and friendly manner					
6.	Overall rating of this instructor(s)					

Comments: _____
_____

Table 12.2 (continued)   LDE Facilitation Feedback Form

Overall Course Evaluation:

Please rate the following items by checking the box that best represents your opinion.

		Rating				
	Item	*Strongly agree*	*Agree*	*Undecided/ neutral*	*Disagree*	*Strongly disagree*
1.	I have a better understanding of the importance of Continuous Improvement.					
2.	I believe that Continuous Improvement will improve my process/job.					
3.	I am confident that Continuous Improvement can be successfully implemented in my process/job.					

Comments: _____
_____

What, if anything, would prevent you from using Continuous Improvement at your job?_____
_____

Please note any additional comments about the course: _____
_____

Thank you!

Chapter 13

The Lean Library

The Lean library provides the needed materials, some that are required for the plant staff and the candidates of the Lean Discipline Expert process and others that are for references and additional education. The Lean library is necessary to support your Lean Discipline Expert program while also offering the opportunity for any of your associates to learn how to apply particular Lean tools to their direct positions—or anyone's position, for that matter.

As mentioned earlier, you should have several Lean Discipline Expert candidates for each subject due to attrition, promotions, etc. Therefore, you will need more than just one copy of each book. The Lean library should operate just as a public library does. There needs to be a central location and a check-out and check-in process for accountability to maintain the investment of the library. If the book somehow cannot be accounted for, then the last person to check it out is responsible to replace it. Each book in the Lean library needs to be numbered. It can be something as simple as 1, 2, 3, or it can be more complicated, such as a sequence of numbers from the ISBN number plus an additional digit. I would recommend that each book have a card with the description of the book, the book's number, and a location for the individual to print his or her name and the date of checkout. The card can simply be placed in a card rack for the visual effect of being able to see what is checked out.

The Lean library does represent an investment, and I usually suggest that the money come from the Human Resource budget, as the books are educational in nature. If you are a corporation with multiple locations around the country or the globe, you will need a Lean library at each site to properly support the Lean Discipline Expert process; sharing among sites not located on the same property just does not work.

Value Stream Mapping
- *Learning To See*; Mike Rother, John Shook; ISBN# 0966784308
- *Seeing the Whole*; Dan Jones, Jim Womack; ISBN# 0966784359
- *The Complete Lean Enterprise*; Beau Keyte, Drew Locher; ISBN# 9781563273018
- *Value Stream Management for the Lean Office*; Don Tapping, Tom Shuker; ISBN# 9781563272462
- *Creating Mix Model Value Streams: Practical Lean Techniques for Building to Demand*; Kevin Duggan; ISBN# 9781439868430
- *Mapping the Total Value Stream: A Comprehensive Guide for Production and Transactional Processes*; Mark A. Nash, Sheila R. Poling; ISBN# 9781563273599
- *Metrics-Based Process Mapping*; Karen Martin, Mike Osterling; ISBN# 9781563273803

5S and Visual Management
- *5S Challenges Video*; Greater Boston Manufacturing Partnership; Bruce Hamilton
- *Who Moved My Cheese? An Amazing Way to Deal with Change in Your Work and in Your Life*; Spencer Johnson, Kenneth H. Blanchard; ISBN# 0091816971
- *Visual Systems: Harnessing the Power of the Visual Workplace*; Gwendolyn D. Galsworth, Anthony Vlamis; ISBN# 0814403204
- *Kamishibai Boards: A Lean Visual Management System That Supports Layered Audits*; Joseph Niederstadt; ISBN# 9781482205299
- *5S for Operators: 5 Pillars of the Visual Workplace*; Hiroyuki Hirano, Melanie Rubin; ISBN# 9781563271236
- *5S for the Office*; Thomas Fabrizio, Don Tapping; ISBN# 9781563273186
- *Gemba Walks for Service Excellence*; Robert Petruska; ISBN# 9781439886748
- *Visual Controls: Applying Visual Management to the Factory Floor*; Chris A. Ortiz, Murry Park; ISBN# 9781439820902
- *The 5S Pocket Guide*; James Peterson, Roland Smith; ISBN# 9780527763381

Standard Work

- *New Manufacturing Challenge: Techniques for Continuous Improvement*; Kiyoshi Suzaki; ISBN# 0029320402
- *Toyota Production System: An Integrated Approach to Just-In-Time*; Yasuhiro Monden; ISBN# 0898061806
- *Standardized Work for Noncyclical Processes*; Joseph Niederstadt; ISBN# 9781439825501
- *New Horizons in Standard Work*; Timothy D. Martin, Jeffery T. Bell; ISBN# 9781439840801
- *Standard Work for the Shop Floor*; Productivity Press Development Team ISBN# 9781563272738

Material Management

- *Toyota Production System: Beyond Large-Scale Production*; Taiichi Ohno; ISBN# 0915299143
- *Kanban for the Shopfloor*; The Productivity Press Development Team; ISBN# 1563272695
- *Creating Level Pull: A Lean Production-System Improvement Guide for Production Control, Operations, and Engineering Professionals*; Art Smalley; ISBN# 0974322504
- *Creating Continuous Flow: An Action Guide for Managers, Engineers & Production Associates*; Mike Rother, Rick Harris; ISBN# 0966784332
- *A Study of the Toyota Production System: From an Industrial Engineering Viewpoint*; Shigeo Shingo, Andrew P. Dillon (Translator); ISBN# 0915299178
- *Making Materials Flow: A Lean Material-Handling Guide for Operations, Production-Control, and Engineering Professionals*; Rick Harris, Chris Harris, and Earl Wilson; ISBN# 0974182494
- *Integrating Kanban with MRPII: Automating a Pull System for Enhanced JIT Inventory Management*; Raymond S. Louis; ISBN# 1563271826
- *Turbo Flow: Using Plan for Every Part (PFEP) to Turbo Charge Your Supply Chain*; Tim Conrad, Robyn Rooks; ISBN# 9781439820674
- *Lean Supply Chain Management Essentials: A Framework for Materials Managers*; Bill Kerber, Brian J. Dreckshage; ISBN# 9781439840825

- *Just-In-Time for Today and Tomorrow*; Taiichi Ohno, Setsuo Mito (Translated by Joseph P. Schmelzeis, Jr.); ISBN# 0915299208
- *Kanban Just-in-Time at Toyota: Management Begins at the Work Place*; Japan Management Association (Translated by David Lu); ISBN# 0915299488
- *Kanban for the Supply Chain: Fundamental Practices for Manufacturing Management*; Stephen Cimorelli; ISBN# 978143989549

Process Problem Solving

- *Continuous Improvement Tools (Quality Improvement Series)*, Vol. 1; Richard Y. Chang, Matthew E. Niedzwiecki; ISBN# 1883553008
- *Continuous Improvement Tools (Quality Improvement Series)*, Vol. 2; Richard Y. Change, Matthew E. Niedzwiecki; ISBN# 1883553016
- *How Toyota Turns Workers into Problem Solvers*; Harvard Business School Article (http://www.hbsworkingknowledge.hbs.edu/pubitem. jhtml?id=2646&sid=0&pid=0&t=operations)
- *Process Problem Solving: A Guide for Maintenance and Operations Teams*; Bob Sproull; ISBN# 9781563272448
- *The Thinker's Toolkit: 14 Powerful Techniques for Problem Solving*; Morgan D. Jones; ISBN# 0812928083
- *8D Process Problem Solving*; www.mindtools.com
- *Problem Solving and Data Analysis Using Minitab: A Clear and Easy Guide to Six Sigma Methodology*; Rehman M. Khan; ISBN# 9781118307571
- *Understanding A3 Thinking: A Critical Component of Toyota's PDCA Management System*; Durward K. Sobek II, Art Smalley; ISBN# 978-1563273605

SMED/Quick Changeover

- *Kaizen for Quick Changeover: Going beyond SMED*; Kenichi Sekine, Keisuke Arai, Bruce Talbot (Translator); ISBN# 0915299380
- *Quick Changeover for Operators: The SMED System* (Shopfloor Series); Productivity Press Development Team; ISBN# 1563271257
- *Quick Response Manufacturing: A Companywide Approach to Reducing Lead Times*; Rajan Suri; ISBN# 1563272016
- *A Revolution in Manufacturing: The SMED System*; Shigeo Shingo; ISBN# 0915299038
- *Kaizen for Quick Changeover: Going beyond SMED*; Keisuke Arai, Kenichi Sekine; ISBN# 9781563273414

Error Proofing

- *Zero Quality Control: Source Inspection and the Poka-Yoke System*; Shigeo Shingo; ISBN# 0915299070
- *Poka-Yoke: Improving Product Quality by Preventing Defects*; Nikkan Kogyo Shimbun; ISBN# 0915299313
- *Mistake-Proofing: Designing Errors Out*; Richard B. Chase, Douglas M. Stewart; ISBN# 978-1438227399
- *Mistake Proofing for Operators*; The Productivity Press Development Team; ISBN# 978-1563271274

TPM

- *Autonomous Maintenance in Seven Steps: Implementing TPM on the Shop Floor*; Masaji Tajiri, Fumio Gotoh; ISBN# 1563272199
- *Autonomous Maintenance for Operators* (Shopfloor Series); The Productivity Press Development Team, Japan Institute of Plant Maintenance (Translated by Andrew P. Dillon); ISBN# 156327082X, 9781563270826
- *Eliminating Minor Stoppages on Automated Lines*; Kikuo Suehiro, Bruce Talbot (Translator); ISBN# 0915299704
- *Implementing TPM: The North American Experience*; Charles J. J. Robinson, Andrew P. Ginder; ISBN# 1563270870
- *Introduction to TPM: Total Productive Maintenance*; Seiichi Nakajima; ISBN# 0915299232
- *TPM for Every Operator* (Shopfloor Series); The Productivity Press Development Team, Japan Institute for Plant Maintenance; ISBN# 1563270803, 9781563270802
- *TPM for the Lean Factory: Innovative Methods and Worksheets for Equipment Management*; Keniche Sekine, Keisuke Arai; ISBN# 1563271915

Continuous Improvement

- *Kaizen Revolution: How to Use Kaizen Events to Implement Lean Manufacturing and Improve Quality, Cost and Delivery*; Michael D. Regan; ISBN# 0966354974
- *Progressive Kaizen: The Key to Gaining a Global Competitive Edge*; John W. Davis; ISBN# 9781439840687
- *The Kaizen Blitz: Accelerating Breakthroughs in Productivity and Performance*; Anthony C. Laraia, Robert W. Hall, Patricia E. Moody; ISBN# 0471246484

- *Kaizen for the Shopfloor*; The Productivity Press Development Team; ISBN# 1563272725
- *The Kaizen Event Planner: Achieving Rapid Improvement in Office, Service and Technical Environments*; Karen Martin, Mike Osterling; ISBN# 9781563273513
- *Kaizen the Art of Creative Thinking*; Shigeo Shingo; ISBN# 978-1897363591
- *Kaizen: The Key to Japan's Competitive Success*; Massaki Imai; ISBN# 9780075543329

Financial

- *Performance Measurement for World Class Manufacturing: A Model for American Companies*; Brian H. Maskell; ISBN# 0915299992
- *Making the Numbers Count: The Management Accountant as Change Agent on the World Class Team*; Brian H. Maskell; ISBN# 1563270706
- *Practical Lean Accounting: A Proven System for Measuring and Managing the Lean Enterprise*; Brian Maskell; ISBN# 9781439817162
- *Lean Accounting Case Studies*; Brian Maskell; ISBN# 9781420084917
- *The Controller as Lean Leader: A Novel on Changing Behavior with a Lean Cost Management System*; Sue Elizabeth Sondergelt; ISBN# 9781439882771

General

- *Contented Cows Give Better Milk: The Plain Truth about Employee Relations and Your Bottom Line*; Bill Catlette, Richard Hadden; ISBN# 890651109
- *America's Best: Industry Week's Guide to World-Class Manufacturing Plants*; Theodore B. Kinni; ISBN# 0471160024
- *The 21 Indispensable Qualities of a Leader: Becoming the Person Others Will Want to Follow*; John C. Maxwell; ISBN# 0785260307
- *Leading the Lean Enterprise*; George Koenigsaecker; ISBN# 9781439859872
- *Understanding Variation: The Key to Managing Chaos* (2nd edition); Donald J. Wheeler; ISBN# 0945320531
- *Knowledge Based Management*; Stephen R. Schmidt, Mark J. Kiemele, Ronald J. Berdine; ISBN# 1880156059
- *Lean Thinking: Banish Waste and Create Wealth in Your Corporation* (revised and updated); James P. Womack, Daniel T. Jones; ISBN# 0743249275

- *Toyota Production System: Beyond Large-Scale Production*; Taiichi Ohno (Foreword by Norman Bodek); ISBN# 0915299143
- *Andy & Me: Crisis and Transformation in the Lean Journey*; Pascal Dennis; ISBN# 9781439825389
- *The Toyota Way: 14 Management Principles from the World's Greatest Manufacturer*; Jeffery K. Liker; ISBN# 9780071392310
- *The Toyota Way to Lean Leadership: Achieving and Sustaining Excellence through Leadership Development*; Jeffery K. Liker, Gary L. Convis; ISBN# 9780071780780
- *Strategic Lean Transformation: Turning Traditional Lean Paradigms into Distinctive Competencies*; Darrell Casey; ISBN# 978-0557060498
- *X Matrix: Strategy Deployment and Execution Process for Breakthrough Business Performance*; Darrell Casey; ISBN# 978-1105370953

Whether you are an individual in the Lean business or a company traveling on your Lean journey, you should have a Lean library. For the individual, of course, it is your decision how small or large of a Lean library to have. But I have found that no matter how proficient you are on Lean practices, once in a while you may need to do some research on a particular subject matter that you haven't utilized in some time.

If you are a company on a Lean journey, in my opinion, it is just common sense to have a Lean library to assist in engaging your associates to become Lean thinkers and change agents on your Lean journey.

Chapter 14

Support Tools for the Visual Factory

I thought it might be helpful to the Lean Discipline Expert candidates to speak about and show examples of tools that I believe they will find helpful to support their visual factory efforts. Your Lean system may already have these incorporated into the various Lean discipline training packages, and if so, by all means use those to remain true to the system standard, but if not, feel free to use these. To build the Lean House you have to have standards, and where there are none you must create them. Only by having standards for everything can you understand what normal versus abnormal conditions are, and I believe we should all understand that when we are on the Gemba, we want to spend our time on the abnormal condition and bring it back to the standard immediately! Another method to help see the normal versus abnormal is through implementing a visual factory with information at the cell, value stream, and/or plant level showing the current status of activities such as trend charts for 5S or changeovers. This ties in directly to the question asked most frequently: "How do I sustain what has been implemented?" The best way I know to maintain and sustain is through layered audits, and the Kamishibai system is one of the best for incorporating layered audits.

These examples are not all-inclusive but will be included on the CRC Press website at http://www.crcpress.com/product/isbn/9781482253658 and will contain blank data points so that you can use your collected real-time data points and insert them into the appropriate space. I believe you will see the value of incorporating these into your visual factory activities.

5S: Workplace Organization: Once you have your 5S standards in place, you need to continually audit to ensure that they are maintained. I believe in an audit that contains a scoring system; once completed, the audit should be reviewed by the 5S Champion with their written comments on the audit, and that document should then be posted in the affected work area. 5S audits should be performed on a regular basis, such as weekly in both the manufacturing (Figure 14.1) and office (Figure 14.2) areas and by personnel not working in the area being audited.

Using a Trend chart (Figure 14.3) or Spider chart (Figure 14.4) to track the progress of an area is another great way to visually check if efforts are going in the right direction, and if they are not, it is time to get working on what needs to be done to correct that negative trend. Again, it is easy to see right away.

The Kamishibai board (Figure 14.5) with 5S task and layered audits cards helps us to see and check—not only on a daily basis, but by shift in areas with multiple shifts—that what is supposed to be done gets done. If it is not being done, create the countermeasure right away. You can also load the Kamishibai board with layered audits for Safety PPE, Standard Work, Autonomous Maintenance, or any category you like. The Kamishibai board works in either manufacturing or office settings, too.

Standard Work—Cyclical: One of the critical tools regarding cyclical standard work is the Work Balance chart (Figure 14.6), for a number of reasons. This chart helps eliminate waste in the process, ensures that work is as evenly distributed as possible between associates, shows that work should be completed within Takt time, and helps the associates see that no one associate is carrying an extra load over the others. In some work environments, it is very important to put that concern to bed. Additionally, it is very important to post the Work Balance chart openly in the area for all to see as part of your visual factory. This will aid the person doing an audit of the standard work to verify that the work sequences and times are being followed. Another is an Hour-by-Hour chart (Figure 14.7). This should also be displayed openly in the work area so that the hourly results can be monitored and the problem resolution verified. There are other tools that you will use in creating cyclical standard work, such as the Time Measurement sheet, Required Associate calculation, Production Capacity, and walk and work-pattern layouts, to name just a few, but you will learn about those and how to apply them during your classroom and hands-on training sessions.

Team/Dept:	Rating					
	0 - Unsatisfactory					
Date of check:	1 - Poor					
	2 - Average					
Overall rating:	3 - Above average					
	4 - Best (sets the example/benchmark)					
Check Item		Evaluation Criteria	Rating				
Sort (Unnecessary Items)			0	1	2	3	4
1	Floor	Free of trash, refuse, proper disposal					
2	Tool benches, tooling	Tooling current, benches free of unnecessary items					
3	Equipment	Free of trash, refuse, extra tooling fixtures and other unnecessary items (i.e., Personal effects)					
4	Cabinets, shelving	Open, free of unnecessary items (i.e., Personal effects)					
5	Information center	Free from trash, refuse, litter					
Straighten (Visual Controls)							
6	Aisles	Marked, maintained, nothing in aisle					
7	Pull storage	I.D., marked, properly stored					
8	Baskets, bins, other containers	Stored, I.D., marked, stacked too high?					
9	Tool benches, boards	Organized, marked, shadow boxes, no blocking fire extinguishers					
10	Information center	Standardized, organized, easy to update					

Figure 14.1 Manufacturing 5S audit form. *(continued)*

Standard Work: Noncyclical: The Yamazumi chart (Figures 14.8 and 14.9) is the perfect tool to graphically see the waste in any noncyclical process. The Yamazumi chart can be prepared by an individual, by individuals across shifts, and by groups across shifts. The tool will also display if the work is balanced or not. With the ability to see these

Check Item		Evaluation Criteria	Rating				
Sweep (Clean)							
11	Floor	Clean, no oil or water stains					
12	Chips, parts, misc.	Contained, stored, nothing scattered					
13	Equipment, tool benches, board	Clean with intent to inspect					
14	Cleaning tools	Handy, organized, stored					
15	Information center	Clean, designated smoking areas					
Sanitize (Maintain)							
16	Visual controls	Maintained					
17	Coolant, oil leaks	Repaired, no bad smell					
18	Lighting	Cleaned, lamps replaced					
19	5S plan	Team map & assignments					
20	Monitoring system	Evidence of team monitoring for compliance					
Sustain (Good Habits)							
21	Safety rules observed	Glasses, hearing protection, lockout, etc.					
22	5S plan display	Team plan in information center, current?					
23	1st 3 5S daily habit	Daily check-off recording					
24	Team involvement	3 shift articulation, advisor on tour					
25	Evaluation results	Displayed in information center - spider chart					

Revision Date: 21Jan14

Figure 14.1 (continued)   Manufacturing 5S audit form.

Plant: _____ Shift: _____ Dept./Area: _____ Date:
_____

		Score	If Score < 4, Indicate Countermeasure, Timing, Resp.
	SCORE: 4 = 100% 3 = 75–99% 2 = 50–74% 1 = 25–49% 0 = 0–24%		
1	Nonusable or excess desks, chairs, tables, filing cabinets, bookcases?		
2	Inoperable projectors, televisions, computers?		
3	Unnecessary reference materials (old reference documents, inactive project binders, obsolete prints)?		
4	Obsolete engineering samples?		
5	Unneeded paperwork, trash?		
6	Permanent items (telephone, computer, calendar, in-out basket, answering machine, personal pictures/items, notepads, etc.) on desk outlined with 1/4" green tape?		
7	Items on floor that move are outlined with 3/4" yellow tape?		
8	Occupant's first and last name posted on the entrance of the cube or on a vertical face of the desk which is easily seen?		
9	No material stored on top of cabinets or desk risers unless there is a logical reason for organizing purposes?		
10	Any productive parts in the office identified per QS9000 procedures?		
11	Tape placed diagonally across books and binders to show when a binder is missing? Related groups are taped together?		
12	Office supply areas store supplies in small plastic bins with contents labeled or use 1/4" green tape to outline the location of the object and label the location?		
13	Reference material is clearly marked and filed?		

Figure 14.2   5S audit form for office. *(continued)*

		Score	If Score < 4, Indicate Countermeasure, Timing, Resp.
14	Shelves, cabinets, closets, and drawers in common storage areas are labeled with their contents?		
15	Supplies are at the point of use (overhead markers by projector, white board markers and erasers by white board, copier supplies by copier)?		
16	Graphic template showing arrangement of conference room posted on the back of conference room doors?		
17	Office layout posted near office entrances?		
18	Sign-in/out boards located close to office entrance?		
19	Desks, tables, file cabinets, white boards, chairs, office equipment (overhead projectors, televisions, fax machines, computers, etc.) are clean/wiped off?		
20	Floors clean?		
21	Lighting adequate?		
22	Per the Clean Desk Policy, all non-permanent items are removed from the desktop at the end of the day (only items marked with green tape are on desktop)?		
23	Tape is replaced on an as-required basis?		
24	Cleaning/maintaining tasks defined and documented on "Clean & Maintain Task Cards"?		
25	Regular audits for 5S & VC conducted by supervisors? Audit results posted?		

Total: _____ = Office 5S Audit Score

Auditors: _____

Figure 14.2 (continued)   5S audit form for office.

things, you will be able to prioritize through a Pareto chart and allocate your resources properly to eliminate waste.

Total Productive Maintenance (TPM): Overall Equipment Effectiveness (OEE), Mean Time To Repair (MTTR), and Mean Time Between Failures (MTBF) are very important measurements in the world of Total Productive Maintenance. It is also important to use the correct formula to measure the OEE of your equipment. It is a combination of Availability, Quality, and Performance, not just one or the other; they must all be considered! To be considered world class, you need to achieve an overall OEE of 85% or better (Figure 14.10).

The formula for calculating MTTR is fairly simple, but you need to collect accurate data: total breakdown time divided by the number of breakdowns. Mean Time To Repair is defined as the average time that it takes to repair something after a failure. So it makes common sense that if you track your OEE and make improvements, your Mean Time To Repair should go down.

The formula for calculating Mean Time Between Failures is also fairly simple, but again you need to be sure to collect accurate data: total operating time divided by the number of breakdowns. Uptime is captured as the moment at which a machine began operating (initially or after a repair) to the moment at which a machine failed after operating. Mean Time Between Failures is literally defined as the average time elapsed from one failure to the next. So, again, it makes common sense that if you track your OEE and make improvements, your Mean Time Between Failures should go up or get longer.

Process Problem Solving: I really like using the A3 format for Process Problem Solving activities (Figure 14.11). There is usually more than one A3 activity going on in manufacturing or business processes at any one time, so this is another great opportunity to post these in a common area for all to see. This makes it easy for teams to meet there to provide verbal updates and to respond to the A3s themselves. I believe that weekly team reviews are ideal. Another great item about a Process Problem Solving A3 is that it walks you through the Plan–Do–Check–Act (PDCA) process (Figure 14.12). People are generally very good with the Plan and Do portions, but they tend to fall flat on the Check and Act portions.

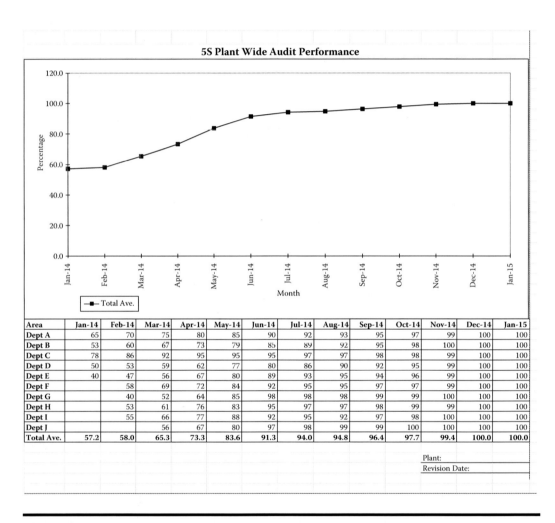

Area	Jan-14	Feb-14	Mar-14	Apr-14	May-14	Jun-14	Jul-14	Aug-14	Sep-14	Oct-14	Nov-14	Dec-14	Jan-15
Dept A	65	70	75	80	85	90	92	93	95	97	99	100	100
Dept B	53	60	67	73	79	85	89	92	95	98	100	100	100
Dept C	78	86	92	95	95	95	97	97	98	98	99	100	100
Dept D	50	53	59	62	77	80	86	90	92	95	99	100	100
Dept E	40	47	56	67	80	89	93	95	94	96	99	100	100
Dept F		58	69	72	84	92	95	95	97	97	99	100	100
Dept G		40	52	64	85	98	98	98	99	99	100	100	100
Dept H		53	61	76	83	95	97	97	98	99	99	100	100
Dept I		55	66	77	88	92	95	92	97	98	100	100	100
Dept J			56	67	80	97	98	99	99	100	100	100	100
Total Ave.	57.2	58.0	65.3	73.3	83.6	91.3	94.0	94.8	96.4	97.7	99.4	100.0	100.0

Plant:
Revision Date:

Figure 14.3   5S Audit Trend chart.

Value Stream:			
5S Category	**2014 Score**	**Goal**	**Statement**
Sort	1.2	*3*	Necessary and unnecessary items have not been separated [including inventory]
Set to Order	1.2	*4*	A designated location has not been established for items
Shine	1.5	*3*	The work area is not cleaned on a regular basis. Key items to visually check have not been identified
Standardize	1.4	*5*	Methods are not being improved and changes are not being documented
Sustain	1.1	*4*	A recognizable effort has not been made to improve the condition of the workarea

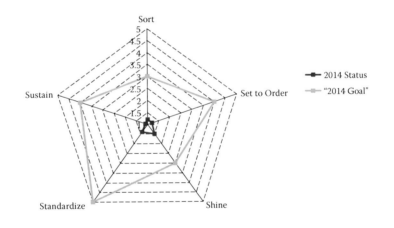

Date:	1/21/2014
Next Posting Date:	2/20/2014

Figure 14.4   5S Audit Spider chart.

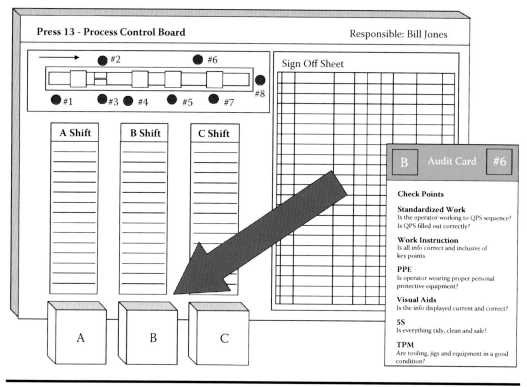

Figure 14.5 Kamishibai board.

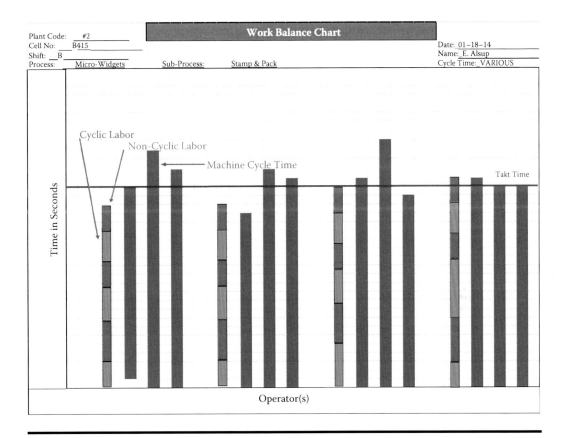

Figure 14.6 Work Balance chart.

Final Assembly					
					HOUR BY HOUR PRODUCTION MONITORING CHART January 23, 2014
A Shift		PIECES			Major Problems
11:00 pm to 7:00am		Good Pieces Assembled			
Hour	Model	Hourly Goal	Hourly count	GAP	
11:00pm - 12:00am	CK20	600	430	170	Tooling Adjustments
12:00am - 1:00am	CK20	600	600	0	
1:00am - 2:00am	CK20	600	600	0	
2:00am - 3:00am	CK20	300	215	85	30 minute lunch 2:00am-2:30am/Power kicked out
3:00am - 4:00am	CK20	600	600	0	
4:00am - 5:00am	CK20	600	200	400	Programmed Tool Change
5:00am - 6:00am	CK20	400	200	200	5:07am-5:30am 23 minute break - Mechanic Needed
6:00am - 7:00am	CK20	600	600	0	
Totals ⟶		4300	3445	855	

Figure 14.7   Hour-by-Hour chart.

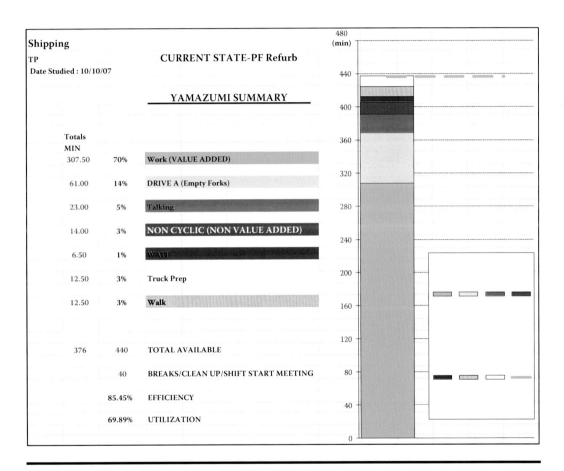

Figure 14.8   Yamazumi individual chart.

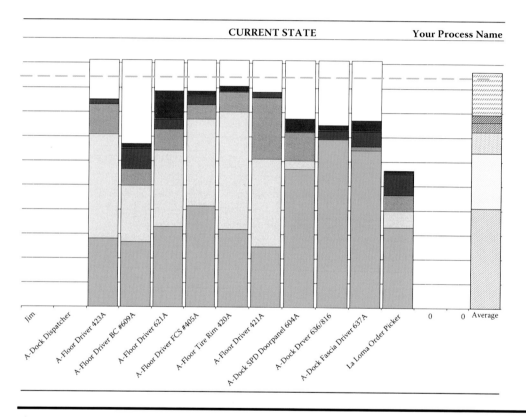

Figure 14.9   Yamazumi group chart.

AVAILABILITY	Equipment/Line/Cell:				1/19/2014	

A. Total Available Time: — 480 Minutes

B. Planned Downtime:

Breaks	20 Minutes	
Lunch	20 Minutes	110 Minutes
Planned Meetings	0 Minutes	
Planned PM	60 Minutes	
Planned GPS Activities	10 Minutes	

C. Net Available Time:
(Total Available Time − Planned Downtime) — 370 Minutes

D. Unplanned Downtime:

	Occurrences	Minutes Lost	
D.1# Start Up	0	0	
D.2 # Breakdowns	0	45	
D.3 # Setups and Adjustments	1	20	
D. 5 # Stock Outages	1	30	101 Minutes
D.6 # Waiting Stock	3	6	
D.7 # Changeovers	0	0	
Total	5	101	

E. Operating Time:
(Net Available Time − Unplanned Downtime) — 269 Minutes

F. Equipment Availability:
(Operating Time divided by Net Available Time) × 100 — 72.70 %

PERFORMANCE EFFICIENCY

G. Total Parts Ran:
(Good and bad parts) — 750 Parts

H. Ideal Cycle Time: — 0.3 Min/Part

J. Performance Efficiency: — 83.64 %
(Ideal Cycle Time × Total Parts Run) divided by Operating Time

Memo:

Documented Blocked/Starved Time

	Occ	Minutes
Blocked	0	0
Starved	0	0

Manpower

Standard	Actual
0	0

QUALITY RATE

K. Total Defects

Rework	Reinspect	Scrap	Defects	
50	0	50	100	100 Parts

L. Quality Rate:
[(Total Parts Ran − Total Defects) divided by Total Parts Ran] × 100 — 86.67 %

OVERALL EQUIPMENT EFFECTIVENESS (OEE)

M. Overall Equipment Effectiveness:
(Equipment Availability × Performance Efficiency × Quality Rate) divided by 10,000 — 52.70 %

MEAN TIME TO REPAIR (MTTR)

Breakdown time Divided by Total Number of Breakdown Occurrences — 0.0 Minutes

MEAN TIME BETWEEN FAILURE (MTBF)

Operating Time Divided by Total Number of Breakdown Occurrences — 269.0 Minutes

Figure 14.10   OEE chart.

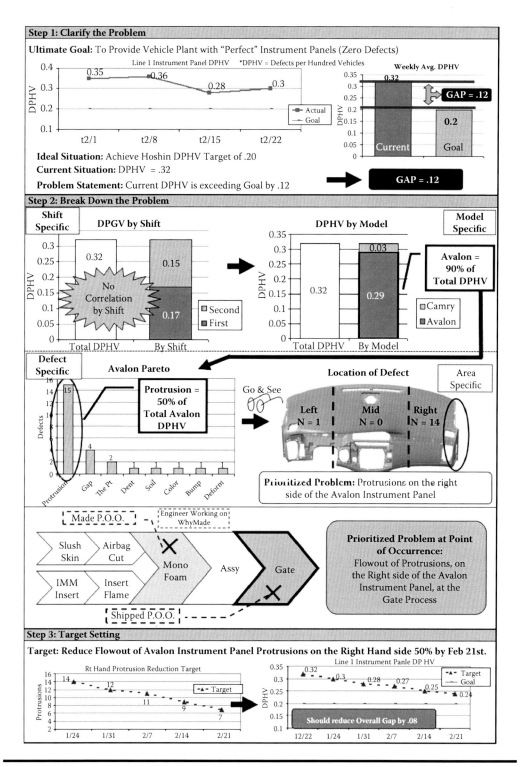

Figure 14.11   Process Problem Solving A3 (continued).

Step 4: Root Cause

Right Hand Protrusion Made

PE Working on Why Made

Why? ⟶

Right Hand Avalon IP Protrusion Shipped

Defect Passed through Gate

TM overlooked Defect

Difficult to see Right Hand Side of Instrument Panel

Material blocking view of Passenger side end panel

Gate Team Member not aware of specific defect area

Poor Jig Design 1

Focus = Why Shipped

STW Followed

Inspection Method No Good ✗

No Specific Feedback Method 2

Go & See

Therefore ⟵

View Obstructed

Listen to Process TM

Step 5: Develop Countermeasures

Root Cause		Countermeasure	Evaluation				
			Cost	Feasibility	Timing	Workability	Priority
1 Poor Jig Design	A	Develop new Jig Style	✗	△	✗	○	NA
	B	Modify Current Jig to Improve Visibility	◬	○	○	○	1
2 No Specific Feedback Method	A	Post large picture of IP at Gate Process with focus area highlighted	○	○	○	○	2
	B	Take pictures of actual defects at offline	○	△	◬	○	3
	C	Post pictures in breakroom/process	○	○	○	○	4

Step 6: See Countermeasures Through

	Countermeasure	Who	When					Status
			1/24	1/31	2/7	2/14	2/21	
1B	Modify Jig	Tool & Die	☆ Implement					●
2A	Post Focus Area at Gate	Eric M.	☆ Implement					●
2B	Take Defect Pictures (negotiate w/Assembly GL)	Eric M.	●······▸			☆ Implement		●
2C	Post Pictures at Process/in Breakroom	Eric M.	●······		······▸		☆	●

●······▸ = Plan
●——▸ = Actual

Step 7: Monitor Results and Processes

Rt Hand Protrusion Reduction Target vs Actual

Protrusions: 16, 14, 12, 10, 8, 6, 4, 2

14 2A
9
8 2B
7 2C
6 6
1B

Countermeasure #2A, B, C Implemented

–▲– Target
–■– Actual

1/24 1/31 2/7 2/14 2/21

6 of 8 days Had Zero Right Hand Protrusion

Countermeasure #1 Implemented

Line 1 Instrument Panel DPHV Target Vs Actual

0.4, 0.3, 0.2, 0.1

Spike From "Other" Defect

0.35 0.36 0.28 0.32 0.3 0.29 0.33 0.3
0.28 0.27 0.26
0.25 0.25 ▲0.24

–▲– Target
–■– Actual
— Goal

t2/1 t2/8 t2/15 t2/22 1/24 1/31 2/7 2/14 2/21

Reduced Overall Gap by .06

Step 8: Standardization

What	How Controlled	Who	Freq.	When
Defect Feedback to Gate TMs	Daily Tracking (Both Shifts) - TM feedback	EM/DE	Daily	On-Going
Notify All Members of Changes	Process Change Form	EM	Once	Jan 25
Yokoten to Instrument Panel Line 2	Meeting with Line 2 Group Leader	EM	Once	Feb 10

Figure 14.11 (continued)   Process Problem Solving A3.

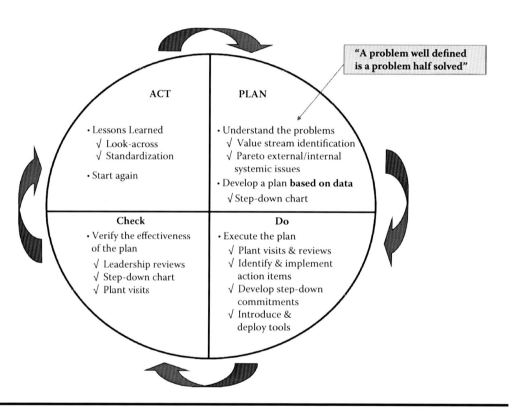

Figure 14.12   Plan–Do–Check–Act process.

Chapter 15

Summary

Well, I certainly believe that you can now see that the Lean Discipline Expert process is very robust and has a lot of "meat on the bones," so to speak. It defnitely takes a commitment on behalf of the organization and the Lean Discipline Expert candidates, but it is well worth it. You should also have a clear understanding of why I mentioned that it generally takes a minimum of two years for a Lean Discipline candidate to reach the expert level. It requires steadfastness and dedication by the Lean Discipline candidate, but the rewards for both the individual and the company are well worth the investment. I have been in several companies that have this system in place, and I can tell you that as soon as you walk in the door, you can just feel a Lean culture in the air. It is even more evident, as you talk with associates at all levels, that everyone has bought into doing and going Lean; they have an army of Lean thinkers. Those two items are the hardest part of implementing Lean: buy-in and culture change.

If you work for a company that truly believes that their biggest asset is their employees, then the Lean Discipline Expert process is ideal for you! If you are a company that does not believe your employees are your biggest asset, you are losing out on a treasure trove of unlimited Lean thinkers.

Appendix: Acronyms

AM: Autonomous Maintenance
CI: Continuous Improvement
EP: Error Proofing
LDA: Lean Discipline Apprentice
LDE: Lean Discipline Expert
LDG: Lean Discipline Generalist
LDS: Lean Discipline Specialist
MM: Material Management
OEE: Overall Equipment Effectiveness
PDCA: Plan–Do–Check–Act
PIT: Process Improvement Team
PM: Preventive Maintenance
PPS: Process Problem Solving
QCO: Quick Changeover
SMED: Single Minute Exchange of Dies
STD: Standard
TPM: Total Productive Maintenance
VM: Visual Management
VSM: Value Stream Mapping
WIP: Work in Process

Index

About the Author

Joseph Niederstadt was born in Saginaw, Michigan, in the early 1950s. This was a town that depended heavily on the automotive industry, as did many towns during this time period. Industry was booming, and mass production was well on the way. The automotive industry employed tens of thousands in the area, providing a standard of living for those working in the factories that few have ever seen or probably will see again.

Like many others in the area, Joe started work in a General Motors factory with the goal of making money and providing benefits for his family yet to come. He never realized that it was the beginning of a career in manufacturing that would span beyond 30 years. His experiences include furnace operator in a foundry, where one job was to rebuild the lining of an electric induction furnace 20 feet from the surface using a 90-pound jackhammer in 100°+ heat (on many occasions, the heat would cause the wood forms he was standing on to catch fire!). Later, he worked at Chevrolet Motor Division and Delphi as an assembly line operator; a water spider on an assembly line; and later moved on to supervise machining, assembly, after-market operations, quality control, production control & logistics, labor relations, Lean core team, supplier development, and international assignments. During this progression, Joe has never forgotten his roots as an operator and has always strived to make the work environment better for the operator.

He has lived through the transition from mass to Lean production, from the "do as I tell you" mentality to a team-managed work system, from massive inventories to Just-in-Time philosophies, from "run all you can every time you can" thinking to Pull systems, from dedicated equipment to flexible cells, from changeovers that took days to those that now take minutes. The list goes on and on. He has been taught by several Senseis from Toyota and some of the best Lean people at other globally renowned and recognized businesses. Joe not only utilizes this training, teaching, and experience in his work, but he has also applied it to his first publication, *Standardized Work for Noncyclical Processes* (CRC Press, 2010), and to this book as well.

Joe has successfully launched Lean journeys and implemented Lean applications throughout the United States, Canada, Mexico, Brazil, Taiwan, India, Korea, China, and Thailand, applying the Kamishibai system presented in this book. He is currently the owner and independent Lean Practitioner at Gemba2win LLC.

In his first book, *Standardized Work for Noncyclical Processes*, Joe provided the reader with a methodology and tools to collect and see data about process waste that is generally overlooked. It is geared for those who wish to take their attack on waste to a new level.

In his second book, *Kamishibai Boards: A Lean Visual Management System That Supports Layered Audits* (CRC Press, 2014), he provided a simple way to see "normal" versus "abnormal" quickly and easily; presented a tool to maintain standards or identify what needs to be returned to standard quickly through visual management; outlined a system to engage all levels in an organization; and described a layered audit process to sustain your organization's implementation of Lean.

In this book, Joe has laid out a process for creating an army of Lean resources for any organization that is willing to make an investment in their associates and a commitment from their leadership.

Remember, your competition hopes you will do nothing!

You can find out more about Joe by viewing his profile on the LinkedIn website.